Technologies of Religion

Bringing together empirical cultural and media studies of religion and critical social theory, *Technologies of Religion: Spheres of the sacred in a post-secular modernity* investigates the powerful entanglement of religion and new media technologies taking place today, taking stock of the repercussions of digital technology and culture on various aspects of religious life and contemporary culture more broadly. Making the argument that religion and new media technologies come together to create "spheres" – environments produced by an architecture of digital technologies of all sorts, from projection screens to social networking sites, the book suggests that prior social scientific conceptions of religious worship, participation, community and membership are being recast. Using the case of the strain of American Christianity called "multi-site," an emergent and growing church-model that has begun to win favor largely among Protestants in the last decade, the book details and examines the way in which this new mode of religiosity bridges the realms of the technological and the physical. Lastly, the book situates and contextualizes these developments within the larger theoretical concerns regarding the place of religion in contemporary capitalism. *Technologies of Religion: Spheres of the sacred in a post-secular modernity* offers an important contribution to the study of religion, media, technology and culture in a post-secular world.

Sam Han is a Seoul-born, New York City-raised interdisciplinary social scientist, working in the areas of social and cultural theory, religion, new media and globalization. He is currently Assistant Professor of Sociology at Nanyang Technological University (NTU) in Singapore and Adjunct Research Fellow at the Hawke Research Institute of the University of South Australia. He is author (with Kamaludeen Mohamed Nasir) of *Digital Culture and Religion in Asia* (Routledge, 2015), *Web 2.0* (Routledge, 2011), *Navigating Technomedia: Caught in the Web* (Rowman & Littlefield, 2007) and editor (with Daniel Chaffee) of *The Race of Time: A Charles Lemert Reader* (Paradigm Publishers, 2009).

Routledge Research in Information Technology and Society

1 Reinventing Government in the Information Age
International practice in IT-enabled public sector reform
Edited by Richard Heeks

2 Information Technology in Government
Britain and America
Helen Margetts

3 Information Society Studies
Alistair S. Duff

4 National Electronic Government
Building an institutional framework for joined up government – a comparative study
Edited by Martin Eifert and Jan Ole Püschel

5 Local Electronic Government
A comparative study
Edited by Helmut Drüke

6 National Governments and Control of the Internet
A digital challenge
Giampiero Giacomello

7 The Politics of Cyberconflict
Security, ethnoreligious and sociopolitical conflicts
Athina Karatzogianni

8 Internet and Society
Social theory in the information age
Christian Fuchs

9 Hacking Capitalism
The Free and Open Source Software Movement
Johan Söderberg

10 Urban Youth in China
Modernity, the Internet and the self
Fengshu Liu

11 Network Governance of Global Religions
Jerusalem, Rome, and Mecca
Michel S. Laguerre

12 Migration, Diaspora and Information Technology in Global Societies
Edited by Leopoldina Fortunati, Raul Pertierra and Jane Vincent

13 A Normative Theory of the Information Society
Alistair S. Duff

14 Is There a Home in Cyberspace?
The Internet in migrants' everyday life and the emergence of global communities
Heike Mónika Greschke

15 Frontiers in New Media Research
Edited by Francis L. F. Lee, Louis Leung, Jack Linchuan Qiu, and Donna S. C. Chu

16 Social Media, Politics and the State
Protests, revolutions, riots, crime and policing in the age of Facebook, Twitter and YouTube
Edited by Daniel Trottier and Christian Fuchs

17 Disorder and the Disinformation Society
The social dynamics of information, networks and software
Jonathan Paul Marshall, James Goodman, Didar Zowghi and Francesca da Rimini

18 Privacy and Capitalism in the Age of Social Media
Sebastian Sevignani

19 Technologies of Religion
Spheres of the sacred in a post-secular modernity
Sam Han

Technologies of Religion
Spheres of the sacred in a post-secular modernity

Sam Han

LONDON AND NEW YORK

First published 2016
by Routledge
2 Park Square, Milton Park, Abingdon, Oxon OX14 4RN

and by Routledge
711 Third Avenue, New York, NY 10017

Routledge is an imprint of the Taylor & Francis Group, an informa business

© 2016 Sam Han

The right of Sam Han to be identified as the author of this work has been asserted by him in accordance with the Copyright, Designs and Patents Act 1988.

All rights reserved. No part of this book may be reprinted or reproduced or utilized in any form or by any electronic, mechanical, or other means, now known or hereafter invented, including photocopying and recording, or in any information storage or retrieval system, without permission in writing from the publishers.

Trademark notice: Product or corporate names may be trademarks or registered trademarks, and are used only for identification and explanation without intent to infringe.

British Library Cataloguing in Publication Data
A catalogue record for this book is available from the British Library

Library of Congress Cataloging in Publication Data
Han, Sam, 1984-
Technologies of religion : spheres of the sacred in a post-secular modernity / Sam Han. -- 1 [edition].
   pages cm. -- (Routledge research in information technology and society ; 19)
Includes bibliographical references and index.
1. Technology--Religious aspects. 2. Digital media--Religious aspects.
I. Title.
   BL265.T4H27 2016
   201'.7--dc23
          2015026633

ISBN: 978-1-138-85586-1 (hbk)
ISBN: 978-1-315-72008-1 (ebk)

Typeset in Times New Roman
by Taylor & Francis Books

Printed and bound by CPI Group (UK) Ltd, Croydon, CR0 4YY

Contents

	Acknowledgements	viii
	Technologies of religion: an introduction	1
1	Disenchantment revisited: formations of the "secular" and "religious" in the technological discourse of modernity	16
2	From cosmos to sphere: "worlds" across religion and technology	29
3	(Atmo)sphere: the liturgical aesthetics of deterritorialized worship spaces	50
4	The digital milieu: the socialization of religious experience in Church Online	74
5	Is the return of religion the return of metaphysics? Or, the renewed spirit of capitalism	90
	Concluding thoughts: reconsidering "the sacred"	108
	References	114
	Index	130

Acknowledgements

A professor once told me, "Writing is fighting." By this, he meant that one needed to have a cause, whether intellectual, political or both (ideally), when he or she engages in writing of any kind. There had to be, in other words, a point to the whole thing, or else it would be a meaningless exercise. I believe he was giving me advice on my honors thesis, which, at the time, lacked an argument. I thank him again for his sage advice.

Many years later, I now understand that it could also mean something rather different. Writing is fighting not only against someone or something but also your self. I am not a good enough writer to feign some kind of romantic suffering that many writers claim to experience. Sadly, not many academics are. However, writing, no matter the writer, does require a sort of effort which to describe in the language of combat is appropriate. Indeed, to read and to think is to open up a Pandora's box overflowing with ideas, arguments, facts, interpretations, myths, fables, etc. These moments of intellectual discovery where all the above collide and morph into sketches of coherence are pure joy, as anyone in the world of letters could attest to. However, the task that so-called academics like myself take on, which is to digest, render intelligible, build upon and organize all of this and to commit to a line of argument (or at least a set of arguments) is tough work. Perhaps I can be accused to overdramatizing but as anyone who has done any sort of writing knows, writing is difficult because it hardly ever mirrors with true fidelity the complexities and nuances of thought that one seems to have. The text is almost always an affront to us.

In spite of this, the publication of this book is one that gives me great satisfaction because of what it represents. Starting out as a doctoral dissertation written while a student at the Graduate Center, City University of New York (CUNY), *Technologies of Religion* is the culmination of five-plus years of learning under and alongside brilliant minds. Although what follows from these pages is quite different from what I handed in many years ago, the influence of the following people can, even now, be seen, and I wish to acknowledge them briefly.

My advisor Patricia Ticineto Clough I cannot thank enough. Having had the fortune of meeting her while still a junior at Wesleyan University, I

Acknowledgements ix

followed her to the Graduate Center to study with her for my doctoral studies. It was a decision I would not regret. Her guidance, sympathy and exacting mind are things I try to mimic with my own graduate students today. Also at the Graduate Center, Stanley Aronowitz and Jerry Watts, whom I also specifically sought after, provided intellectual inspiration and support. To have scholars of their stature have my back as a graduate student gave me the confidence I needed to pursue my rather varied and, sometimes unusual, interests—without apology. Additionally, I learned a great deal about religion from others at the GC, especially Bryan Turner, Talal Asad and John D. Boy.

My thinking about religion, media and digital culture was inspired by scholars such as Heidi Campbell, Christopher Helland, Stewart Hoover and Jeremy Stolow, all of whom I had the fortune of meeting at various conferences and workshops where ideas contained in this book were discussed and sharpened. My thanks to them and organizers of these events, especially Nabil Echchaibi, Tim Hutchings, Faye Ginsburg, Pegi Vail and Angelia Zito. I have also benefitted greatly from conversations with a great number of scholars on issues discussed in this book. I will just briefly mention here Alexandra Boutros, Kyuhoon Cho, Stefan Gelfgren, Jin Kyu Park, and Babak Rahimi.

At Routledge, Simon Bates, Yuvaneswari Yogaraja and Sabrina Lacey were crucial in bringing this project to fruition. Jaya Chowdhury provided excellent copy-editing.

At Nanyang Technological University (NTU), Singapore, I must thank members the faculty and administrative staff of the Division of Sociology for sustaining a wonderful environment to be a scholar and teacher. I'm happy to call it home.

It is with my grandmother, aunt, parents and brother, the now *Pastor* Paul Han, on our weekly trips to church and other excursions to different Korean congregations in the Bronx and the greater New York metropolitan area, that I began to observe the relationship between technology and religion. I thank them for dragging me around back then. Without my wife Zarelda Marie Goh, who is always on the same team as me, neither this book nor much else would be possible.

I must also acknowledge the different places that portions of this book have made earlier appearances. Chunks of chapter 1 appeared in *Social Compass* 62:1, 2015, and small bits of Chapter 3 were published in *Reviews in Cultural Theory* 4:1, 2013.

Readers of this book will also find resonant points between this work and another—the just recently published *Digital Culture and Religion in Asia* (Routledge, 2015). While I lack the audacity to envision this as a work of multiple volumes, I encourage readers to view them as companions.

While I relied upon the efforts of so many, the unavoidable limitations and errors found in this book are but my own.

Sam Han
Singapore

Technologies of religion
An introduction

"Using the Internet can destroy your faith." That is exactly what an article on the website of the *MIT Technology Review* stated in its very first sentence. Detailing a study that had just been released, the article assesses the claims made by a computer scientist analyzing data from the General Social Survey, one of the most trusted quantitative social science databases in America. Since 1990, there has been a dramatic drop in religious affiliation in the United States while, in that same period, there has been an increase in Internet use. This correlation, according to the study, demonstrates "the increase of Internet use in the last two decades has caused a significant drop in religious affiliation" (arXiv 2014). Putting aside the difference between causation and correlation, it may be useful to just explore a bit of the argument.

As has been rather widely accepted among quantitative social scientific studies of religion, in the United States, the biggest influence on religious affiliation is whether one was brought up in a certain religion. Those that were are more likely to identify themselves as adherents later in life. Starting in the 1980s, both numbers began to drop. Those who had a stated religious affiliation as well as those who reported a religious upbringing declined steadily. Indeed, the accepted explanation was precisely to link these two drops. However, it did not explain all of the decline in religious affiliation. Another factor that many social scientists of religion pointed to was the rise in education. While this too was found to be a significant factor, it only accounted for 5 percent of the drop in religious affiliation. There must be another factor.

To fill this explanatory void, Allen Downey, the computer scientist, introduces the variable of Internet use. In the 1980s, when the declines in religious affiliation were first noticed, there was no widespread Internet use. By 2010, the numbers, as expected, are quite extraordinary. Fifty-three percent of the population spends at least two hours online and 25 percent spends at least seven hours. Now, just because we see two phenomena taking place concurrently does not mean there is a relationship between the two. There is no overtly obvious connection but Downey concludes that there is one. His rather telling explanation hinges on the concepts of homogeneity and heterogeneity. As he notes, "for people living in homogeneous communities, the Internet provides opportunities to find information about people of other

2   *Technologies of religion*

religions (and none), and to interact with them personally...Conversely, it is harder (but not impossible) to imagine plausible reasons why disaffiliation might cause increased Internet use" (arXiv 2014).

When looking deeper into the logic of the arguments made in the study, a general image of the currently dominant ideas regarding religiosity, secularity, and media technology, specifically the Internet, can be gleaned. As the opportunity grows for encountering and engaging with different ideas and people, religious affiliation will undoubtedly decrease. The lack of depth in this sort of explanation is one that is revealing not of any sort of limitation of the investigator or the study itself. Indeed, there are many studies and reports that operate under this sort of analytic rubric. But I would like to suggest that these narratives and assumptions are part of the larger story of modernity, specifically "secular modernity," where modern culture, and its cultural and ethical values of self-origination, freedom, creativity, self-liberation and self-making, is unduly tied to the nebulous idea of the secular (Gillespie 2008: 2). What is the secular? What is its relationship to the religious? What is its relationship to technology and media? These questions will be explored in greater detail in the following chapter. For now though we can simply sketch a conceptual schema where "secularity" deems religion and media technology are thought to be simply incompatible, or at least an awkward fit.

The discussions in critical social theory debating the place of religion in modernity have been going on for at least two decades. Since the "turn to religion" in the 1990s (de Vries 1999), there has been no shortage of publications assessing various religious traditions and phenomena and how they fit into what was once called the "secularization thesis," which viewed the institutional transformations of modernity such as individualization, bureaucratization, and industrialization, to name but a few, as ultimately chipping away many aspects of tradition, chiefly religion. While secularization theory is no longer in fashion, the question of religion's place in largely secular modernity still haunts the many works that have emerged in the wake of the religious turn. This can be seen in a range of scholarly contributions in this vein, from those that deal with the commensurability of religion with modern liberal democracy, such as the politics of the hijab in Europe, to others on the growing visibility of religious interest groups in the politics of the nation-state globally. While this area of scholarship has produced very important work, offering up very useful concepts such as "post-secular modernity," which certainly has abiding relevance in the contemporary world experiencing a so-called religious revival, it has not factored in one of the most important changes to come about in roughly that same period of social theory's supposed "religious turn" – namely, the information revolution. Sitting, as we do now, on the cusp of the "internet of things" and "Web 3.0," where so many aspects of contemporary social and political life happen digitally on our growing ecology of interoperable mobile devices, it seems that to reckon with the consequences of new media technologies on religion is necessary to understand what "the secular" as well "as the religious" mean today.

Technologies of religion 3

In the popular press, stories with headlines such as "Our Father, Lead Us to Tweet, and Forgive the Trespassers," to mention but one instance, are no longer to be met with surprise (Vitello 2009). Detailing various attempts by Jewish, Christian, and Muslim congregations to incorporate Twitter, the article highlights some issues, especially around control, raised when religion and media technologies converge. One telling example concerned a Protestant church in Michigan. While experimenting with projecting the live stream of tweets from the congregation behind the pulpit during the worship service, there were some stray comments such as "Nice shirt, pastor!" and "Jesus is a joke." In spite of this, the article reports that faith leaders err on the side of new media. "If someone chooses to interact with us mischievously, that's fine. The opposite of engagement is not mischief, but apathy," a pastor is quoted as stating.

While this attention to matters religious and digital offers evidence of a "post-secular age," that is, an age where the modern and the religious can be imagined to coexist, both scholarly and popular accounts of these phenomena, however, reflect the all-too-common understanding of the relationship of religion and technologies as still incommensurable, or at best, awkward. This stems from the association of the former with the historical past, or tradition, and the latter with the present, or modernity. Furthermore, what is also detectable is what Heidegger once called the "anthropological" or instrumental view of technology, that is, technology as mere tools for human use. This theory of technology strips away its power, its ontology, and fails to acknowledge that media and technology, when used by humans, also exert their force, their power, on the users. Unfortunately, we can see aspects of this rather limited view in other areas of scholarship as well. In the sociology of religion, studies on contemporary Christianity, including congregational studies on megachurches, for instance, merely mention the inclusion of technologies such as projection screens, satellite video, audio rigs, involved in churches today but do not go on to assess fully their impact on the fundamental analytic categories of the field such as participation, community and space. Likewise, in media studies as well as science and technology studies (STS), religion barely registers as a topic of inquiry although some scholars tip their hats to religion as that which preceded science's ultimate epistemological dominance.

Religion within the limits of secular reason alone

So how does it follow that the secular pits religion and technology against one another? While this is the subject of chapter 1, for now, we can simply start from the fact that technology is an extension of scientific knowledge, one of the hallmarks of the Enlightenment. The discipline of sociology, emerging in nineteenth-century Europe, of course is steeped in the principles of the Enlightenment project (Shilling and Mellor 2001: 5–10). Many historical accounts of sociology's intellectual formation agree that its treatment of religion reveals much about its relationship to Enlightenment thought. In both the French and German tradition of sociology, religion is understood on a moral

4 *Technologies of religion*

basis. In the French traditions of Durkheim and Comte, religion has a major role in providing society with a moral code. Shilling and Mellor argue that this amounts to a position between the Enlightenment and counter-Enlightenment, with "society" amounting to a religious phenomena. This is the religion of humanity and God being society itself. To the contrary, the German tradition understood religion as affecting the moral capacities of individuals not the moral order of society. Weber and Simmel, Shilling and Mellor's representative German classical social theorists, both understood religion in relation to the individual and his or her moral orientation and capacity to tell the difference between good and evil. For Simmel, religion satiated the human need for the experience of transcendence while Weber thought it provided meaning for individuals. In modernity, neither thought there was much hope for religion as previously constituted (Shilling and Mellor 2001: 10).

The "moral basis" of religion in turn-of-the-century social thought brought forth, however, a modern metaphysics in a theoretical project which was supposed to spurn any sort of relic of superstition. This argument, made prominent by the theologian John Milbank, problematizes the concept of "the social" and "society", calling it a "theology." The category of the social provides a backdrop, a universal and ahistorical one, which precedes all, including politics or individual morality. It is "a set of social facts and laws prior to virtue and prior to the setting of goals of action," as he writes. It acts similarly as the Christian concept of "providential design" with the individual "always already situated within society." Society, therefore, is the basis for all behavior, including religious behavior. Religion as such attains the status of the Kantian sublime: "a realm of ineffable majesty beyond the bounds of the possibility of theoretical knowledge, a domain which cannot be imaginatively represented, and yet whose overwhelming presence can be acknowledged by our presence of freedom, of the soul, the transcendental 'apperceived' self, and therefore of irreducible humanity" (Milbank 1990: 104). The conditions of religion, this sublime, are already given by the social as either "factual a priori or as a priori norm." It is cocooned and protected. Or, to put it more strongly, as Milbank does, sociology has policed the sublime by relegating religion as a "component of the protected 'human' sphere ... kept rigorously behind the bounds of the possibility of empirical understanding" (Milbank 1990: 106). On the rare occasion that religion is evoked, sociology makes it so that it is either "purely instrumental and goalless rationality" or the reason behind "ultimate political purpose," such as in the case of religious politics (Milbank 1990: 106). Thus, we can say, after Milbank, that the very analytic basis of the discipline of sociology, and with it classical social theory – that is, the idea of the "social – exists 'within the history of 'the secular'" as a means of self-legitimation and as part of "its attempt to legitimate itself, and to 'cope' with the phenomenon of religion" (Milbank 1990: 102).

From the earliest days of its formation following the Enlightenment, sociology and social theory *constructed* religion wholly in secular, that is, functionalist, terms. The beginnings of modern social thought are crucial to

Technologies of religion 5

understanding that the social as such is a way of conceptually dealing with religion in modern terms. As Milbank notes, the constitution of religion in secular terms carries right through to contemporary social science and social theory. As a matter of fact, according to him, the clearest demonstration of this trend is in the sociology of religion, which incorporates all of sociology's secular biases in order to study religion. In effect, he argues that the sociology of religion that comes after Parsons (including Robert Bellah, Peter Berger, and Clifford Geertz) all falls in a trap of burdening religion with either an instrumentality or ultimate political rationality, and sometimes both. Religion is at once charismatic and existential and also integrative, contributing to the construction and maintenance of the social order (Milbank 1990: 109). Just for convenience's sake, we can look at Clifford Geertz's "Religion as a Cultural System," where Geertz famously argues for a meaning-oriented understanding of religion. We can see rather clearly the argument that Milbank makes. For Geertz, religion keeps the chaos of life at bay. It is a way of *explaining* paradox, mystery, and death. But additionally, it also asserts order.

> Religion is: (1) a system of symbols which acts to (2) establish powerful, pervasive, and long lasting moods and motivations in men by (3) formulating conceptions of a general order of existence and (4) clothing these conceptions with such an aura of factuality that (5) the moods and motivations seem uniquely realistic.
>
> (Geertz 2004: 4)

Indeed Geertz's focus is on the ability of religion to construct a world of *meaning*. He describes this process, not coincidentally in my view, in technological terms (e.g., "sources of information," "model") (Geertz 2004: 7). The goal of religion, he suggests, is to formulate:

> by means of symbols, [an] image of such a genuine order of the world which will account for, and even celebrate, the perceived ambiguities, puzzles and paradoxes in human experience. The effort is not to deny the undeniable – that there are unexplained events, that life hurts or that rain falls upon the just – but to deny that there are inexplicable events, that life is unendurable and that justice is a mirage ... What is important, to a religious man at least, is that this elusiveness be accounted for, that it be not the result of the fact that there are no such principles, explanations or forms, that life is a surd and the attempt to make moral, intellectual or emotional sense out of experience is bootless.
>
> (Geertz 2004: 23)

While critics of Milbank accuse him of misreading sociology and social theory, there are card-carrying social scientists of religion who have argued similarly. In critiquing the "insular" nature of the sociology of religion in the mid-1980s, the sociologist James Beckford suggested that the dominant

6 Technologies of religion

approach in the field, which he labels "functionalist phenomenology" characterized by "the adoption of a kind of phenomenological and cognitive sociology," had "relegated the significance of religion to that of one among many functional meaning-systems generated in the course of social interaction" (Beckford 1985: 350).

Additionally, the anthropologist Talal Asad has argued that Geertz's definition of religion as a cultural system wrongly assumes that "human beings have a deep dread of disorder." Religious symbols, according to this formulation, fulfill the "profound need for a general order of existence" (Asad 1993: 45). If that is the case, then, as Asad argues, Geertz's conception of religion resembles that of Marx's thesis of religion as *ideology* – "that is, as a model of consciousness which is other than consciousness of reality, external to the relations of production, producing no knowledge, but expressing at once the anguish of the oppressed and a spurious consolation" (Asad 1993: 46). Although Geertz's definition provides analytic resources for the study of religion, some of which this book draws from, I believe, in agreement with Milbank and Asad, it recapitulates the restricted definition of religion in modern social theory, and especially the sociology of religion, and therefore is ensnared by similar issues. Rather expectedly, this has left an impression on the study of religion, media and culture as well. With very little exception, these studies proceed without acknowledging the modern and secular conditions that constitute the very phenomena they study.

Working through cultural and media studies of religion

The works of scholarship that have emerged in the past decade analyzing religion and media are numerous, stretching across disciplinary boundaries as well as theoretical and methodological proclivities. To attempt to give a full overview of these developments would be neither appropriate nor necessary as it has already been done, and done well (see Campbell 2012; Stout 2011; Mahan 2014). These works, which I place under the title of "cultural and media studies of religion," have in common the shared intention of demonstrating the significance of new media and communications technologies in the "comeback in sociological and anthropological literature" experienced by religion (de Vries 2002: 6). I give a brief account of some major argumentative and theoretical threads in order to situate the current project.

There are works that are situated as cultural studies of religion. Many of these works offer rich, detailed accounts of the interfacing of popular culture and religion. For instance, in *Shaking the World for Jesus*, Heather Hendershot's book on contemporary evangelical Christian media, she argues that much of the cultural rapprochement of evangelical Christianity with secular, mainstream culture is, at most, "ambiguous." "Evangelicals," she writes, "repeatedly [draw] on previously existing [secular, mainstream cultural] forms, often turning them completely on their ear, as in antimarijuana reggae songs or rock tunes advocating submission to parents" (Hendershot 2004: 13). As Hendershot

Technologies of religion 7

shows through various examples, reports of incommensurability between *secular* culture and *religious* media are wildly exaggerated. This is due to the fact that Christian media in particular attempts to "somehow provide pleasure (since kids won't consume media they find dull)" while maintaining its Christian aspect (Hendershot 2004: 37). Hence, she concludes, there is no outright "resistance" to mass culture on the part of evangelical Christian media but rather an acknowledgment that it must be dealt with. As can be seen, this sort of approach does not fully immerse itself in the media of which it speaks. Media become mere conduits of culture or "the mainstream." What is missing is a greater appreciation of the ways in which the technological aspects of communications media affect religious practice, authority, and community.

Scholars of what is called "digital religion" do precisely this. When looking at the work of perhaps the most important scholar in this regard, Heidi Campbell, we can see a detailed focus of the media at play. Campbell is greatly influenced by "the social-shaping of technology" approach and forges what she calls the "religious-social shaping of technology" approach.

> A unique element of the religious-social shaping of the technology is that it seeks to explore in more detail how spiritual, moral, and theological codes of practice guide technological negotiation. Thus, it calls for a deeper awareness of the role history and tradition play in religious communities' process of negotiation. This means not only looking at what contemporary values and beliefs shape motivations related to technology use, but also uncovering the historical roots and rhetoric of these discourses in a given religious community.
>
> (Campbell 2010: 59)

Campbell's work, it can be said, has set both the theoretical and methodological agenda for studies of religion, media, and culture. However, what is somewhat absent in her work is an engagement with critical social theory, that is, of larger debates surrounding secularism and modernity but also new media theory, which would crucially situate their robust empirical findings in aesthetic and other cultural contexts.

This has been addressed somewhat by "media anthropology," which has done much work to address, for instance, matters of embodiment and sensation, especially vision, with regard to phenomena such as televangelism. The key works not only combine theoretical rigor and empirical substance, but also engage theologically with their respective religious specializations. Take, for instance, the work of Birgit Meyer, who has explored the entanglement of religion and media as *not* an instance of religion simply utilizing media. But rather, she insists that religion itself is a "practice of mediation" in the broadest sense, involving all sorts of means of closing the "distance between human beings in the world and the divine realm." The recent meeting of religion and new media then is a "new moment" in the greater history of mediation (Meyer 2006:

8   Technologies of religion

435). Thus, when looking at the religious incorporation of new media, "it is never just a matter of adopting or adapting to a new technology." Rather, "in order to function in religious mediation practices, such a new technology needs to be authorized as suitable means to merge with what it sets out to mediate" (Meyer 2006: 437). One of the merits of this particular approach is the sensitivity to how media and religion are both *modes of representation*.

Media anthropology and digital religion, however, remain well within the framework of "institutional" religion. The emergence of new religious movements, as well as the rise of alternative spirituality, have also provided a great deal of empirical cases for scholars studying media, culture, and religion. For the study of religion and the Internet, neo-paganism holds a special place. It is the subject of some of the earliest studies, including that of Stephen O'Leary as well as Gregory Grieve. O'Leary's article is credited with laying out the first sketches of what is called "online religion," a term which held a great deal of influence for quite some time, until, one could say, the clarifications provided by the work of Christopher Helland, who distinguished it from that of "religion online." What makes this line of scholarship so important, besides the fact that it was pioneering, is that it argued for the importance of the "online-ness" of "online religion," meaning that the way religion was thought of and practiced was impacted by its occurrence on the Internet. The dynamics of interaction and communication that were unique to the Internet at the time – its reliance on text, for instance – could not be dismissed. The rituals, while performed with a keyboard, screens, and a mouse, were still ritual and helped religious communities come to life and construct a "virtual reality" that rivaled real-life religion. Ritual was not strictly action any more. It was now simulations (O'Leary 2004: 49). This fact, however, does not take away from the efficacy of online religion. At the same time, online religion is not attempting to "recreate" the effects of religion by reproducing the material aspects of ritual. Instead, O'Leary argues, the constructed and artificial quality of the online rituals is part and parcel of the experience and actually does not hinder the ultimate aim of all ritual, which is to "restructur[e] and reintegrat[e] the minds and emotions of their participants" (O'Leary 2004: 56).

Yet, as Campbell notes, in her commentary on O'Leary, his argument amounts to proving that online religion *is* religion. In spite of all the technological and communicational newness, what is occurring within neo-pagan communities on the Internet are nothing but "cyber-rituals." By attempting to draw a connection between religious practice online and offline, we end up with the rather difficult, and often times tenuous, balancing act of maintaining the uniqueness of the online experience for online religion but still also using well worn interpretive frameworks of social science such as *ritual*. Is online religion the mere movement of religion to new media?

An additional approach, which has gathered much critical attention, comes from scholars in Scandinavia, who have coined the term "mediatization." They answer the question by suggesting that today media affects everything, forcing other spheres of life to yield to its frameworks and logics. Stig

Technologies of religion 9

Hjarvard, who is the most identifiable figure using this approach, dubs mediatization of religion as a "theory of the media as agents of religious change" (Hjarvard 2008). By "mediatization," Hjarvard refers to the process where "the media" as an independent institution, is increasingly relied upon by other social institutions such as the economy and politics in order to communicate with one another but also society at large. He describes this reliance as "[having] to accommodate the *logic* of the media" (Hjarvard 2008: 11, emphasis added). Thus, religion, as another institution of society, must submit itself to media's whim – its technological features, aesthetic features, and institutional frameworks. Hjarvard even uses the word "subsume" to describe this process (Hjarvard 2008: 14). In the case of religion specifically Hjarvard points out that media acts upon religion via an impact on "the amount, content and direction of religious messages in society" while also affecting religious representations and mounting a challenge, and even threatening to replace, the authority of institutional religion (Hjarvard 2008: 14). As an example, he points to religious representations such as "crosses, prayers and cowls" that now are no longer tied to Christianity necessarily (Hjarvard 2008: 15). In the recent history of hip hop, the "Jesus Piece," a gold chain with a pendant in the shape of the face of Jesus, usually made of gold and encrusted in gems such as diamonds, was a hot commodity, with Kanye West, Jay-Z, and the late-Notorious B.I.G. wearing them as did others whose religious affiliations were not necessarily known to be Christian. Thus, the main effect, so to speak, of "mediatization" is "banalization." Media, as "embedded in every-day routines," allows for religious symbols and messages to be part of the daily experience of living as opposed to a transcendent and even sacred, set of representations. Religion is not eliminated but rather transformed.

All of these various approaches to the study of media, religion and culture, while sharing some aspects are also rather different to one another, especially when looking at what they judge to be the *effects* of the ever-increasing entanglement of religion and media. How they see this relationship, of course, is greatly influenced by the conceptualization of the very terms religion, media, and culture. In the case of the cultural studies of religion, there is a concerted effort to diminish the incommensurability of "the religious" and "the secular" by showing that there is strong cultural engagement on the part of religion with secular, mainstream culture. With the religious-social shaping approach, there is an emphasis on negotiation. If indeed a religious group decides to adopt a particular medium or technology, it does so based on its own needs and motives. What is emphasized is that religion and media do not simply interact through "use," but rather through strategic attempts at leveraging certain aspects of the religious community. "Religion" is not taken as a given here. To the contrary, in media anthropology, "media" is not taken as an extant entity. According to this line of thought, media, digital media especially, has a certain way of affecting sensation, allowing it to reproduce in some fashion "immediate experience." Religion, in some ways, also attempts to do this through various practices involving ritual. Indeed the meeting place of religion and media are

10 *Technologies of religion*

in the body. Online religion places greater emphasis on the technological aspects of media. Stressing the way in which performing rituals on the Internet maintains the end-goals of ritual, the online religion approach insists upon the religiosity of online religion. "Mediatization" operates from a counter-position. Insisting on media's hegemony, all "institutions" of society, including religion, adhere to its logic and are thus necessarily changed by it.

Very few of these studies, however, situate their positions vis-à-vis modernity and secularism. Specifically, their understanding of modernity, and its relationship to the secular, necessarily provides the theoretical background, or the condition of possibility, for the very concepts that they aim to explore, to wit, media, religion, and culture. Returning to "mediatization," for the sake of convenience and also because it is the analytic that has received most attention recently, we see that Hjarvard's argument is rooted in an understanding of the current era as differentiated into spheres, which he labels "institutions." This is, in a sense, already a secularized understanding of modernity. As the following chapter will discuss further, differentiation, the idea that society will continue to be rationalized into categorical entities, is one of the hallmarks of secularization theory. Furthermore, if indeed Hjarvard's argument depends upon media "infecting" others in the contemporary era, it follows, then, that there are separate institutions that existed *outside* of media at one point although they no longer do. The question then becomes whether media ever existed independently, as Hjarvard likes to say. Could not one argue that the sphere of politics was always dependent upon and relied on media of some kind or another? One need not look any further than Habermas and Anderson to see ample evidence of this. The same can go for "religion," which of course stands as an institution that was, at one point, independent of media. Yet, how could one discuss the Protestant Reformation without the Gutenberg printing press?

I raise these questions not with the intent of critiquing "mediatization" or any of the other approaches discussed briefly above in detail. Rather, I do so in order to point out the fact that in cultural and media studies of religion, while the terms "religion," "media," "technology," and "culture" are scrutinized in relation to one another, they are treated as given and not interrogated from the perspective of modernity. One may ask why this would be important. An objection could be raised with regard to depth and specificity. In other words, by viewing recent developments in religion and media through a larger, perhaps more general, lens, do we not sacrifice detail? Are there not enough studies that remain at the level of generality and abstraction and lack empirical specificity? I contend, through this book, that this need not be the case. By engaging in critical social theory, especially the debates surrounding secularism and modernity, cultural and media studies of religion would benefit from this recalibration. The impetus behind this is not some sense of "balance," which, for a brief moment, held purchase in the social sciences, particularly in the form of "grounded theory," or its forebear "middle range theory."

To the contrary, the purpose of such a move is to conduct analyses of religion, media, and culture while being clear about the current situation, not place these terms in a hermeneutic vacuum. Religion, media, and technology are all constituted by modernity. These are loaded terms obviously – today more than ever. This book, unfortunately, will not provide definitive meanings to any of them – on purpose. It is the task, I believe, for studies of media, religion, and culture to *create* concepts, to quote Deleuze and Guattari. By creation, they do not mean "to make up" out of thin air. Instead, much in the way Deleuze (with exception to his collaborative works with Guattari) wrote philosophy *through* other thinkers, such as in his works on Kant, Nietzsche, and Foucault, to create concepts is not to sidestep what has come before but to "work through" it, in the sense of Freud. In "Remembering, repeating and working-through" (1914), Freud succinctly describes the therapeutic process of psychoanalysis. He attempts to make a clear distinction between repeating and remembering. The former is the source of neurosis. Repeating is the symptom of the psyche's inability to properly cope with something. It is the sign of "resistance," as Freud says, to the therapeutic process. Thus the compulsion to repeat indicates repression. Remembering, on the other hand, is what the analyst is attempting to achieve in the analysand, or the patient. But how is that done? Freud provides a relatively simple answer: working through it, overcoming it, and continuing the analytic work. Remembering and repeating offer different relationships between the psyche and what Freud calls "the original situation," a trauma or something similar. Remembering allows for *interpretation*, which Freud associates with verbalization of the memory, or trauma, in the analytic setting. Repetition is merely compulsion. There is no room for interpreting. The memory, or at least the psyche's version of the memory, is stuck in a loop.

The psychoanalytic concepts of remembering, repeating, and working-through have some lessons for the study of religion, media, and culture but also social theory and social science more broadly. To repeat without remembering is to give up on one of the most powerful tools of social thought, which is interpretation, that is, working-through. Hence, this book, again, while it will surely disappoint those who are seeking a type of study with clear definitions of "religion" and "technology," attempts to *work through* previous work on religion, media, and culture although it is not wholly animated by the psychoanalytic method. By working through, I mean that it seeks to address, incorporate, and create new concepts out of tried and true analytics that have come from the broad range of scholarly literatures that this book situates itself in, including sociology, anthropology, media studies, and critical social theory.

Technologies of religion

Bringing together empirical work done in the vein of the emergent field of the cultural and media studies of religion with larger social-theoretical discussions on secularism and modernity, this is a book that investigates the entanglement of religion and new media technologies, taking stock of the repercussions of

12 Technologies of religion

both digital culture and technology on various aspects of religious life, specifically worship and community, as they have been recast to emphasize themes of embodiment, affectivity, and sociality. *Technologies of Religion* makes the argument that religion and new media technologies come together to create "spheres," digital environments that recast prior theological definitions of religious participation and community. Using the case of the strain of American Christianity called "multi-site," an emergent and growing church-model that has begun to win favor largely among Protestants in the last decade, which refers to churches that have a central location and many "satellite campuses" and distinguished by heavy use of digital technologies, such as "simulcasting" worship services in addition to the online ministry such as online church, podcasts, email, and social networking site presence among other things, the book details and examines the way in which this new mode of religiosity bridges the realms of the technological and the physical. The book connects this empirical instance of contemporary digital-religious culture and practice with the larger theoretical concerns regarding the place of religion in today's post-secular, post-modernity.

Using Christian-oriented technology publications, interviews, and participant-observation as data, I study and analyze specifically the digital aspects of contemporary Christianity in order to contribute to a better understanding of the increasingly technological nature of multisite Christianity in America today. In doing so, I am influenced by two "methodological" approaches in the main. I put "methodological" here in scare quotes because part of the project of this work is to subvert the dominant duality of theory and method which characterizes most of social science research today. I view this work to be both a work of theory and a work of empirical research. At any rate, analytically, this book sits between STS (science, technology, and society) and multisite ethnography.

Specifically, I draw from the work of scholar John Law, who has called for "a better tuned" method (or better yet, a "post-method") that pushes "singularity" toward "multiplicity." Social science, for the most part, sees the "social" as determined, confined, a similar analysis as Milbank. In turn, it assumes that there are "definite processes out there waiting to be discovered." The task of social scientific method, then, is to aid in the "[discovery of] the most important of those definite processes" (Law 2004: 6–7). Law calls this the "concern of method of its inheritance with hygiene" (2004: 9). But what if, as Law suggests, the world, or the social, is not so definite but rather an "unformed" and "generative flux of forces and relations that produce particular realities" (2004: 7)?

For Law, the world no longer resembles enclosure, as social science for so long assumed. In light of this, method would necessarily have to shift from a position vis-à-vis reality consisting mainly of discovery and depiction, which becomes decreasingly appropriate as "reality," according to Law, is hardly ever fully formed, not to mention singular. It would move, instead, toward what he describes as "the enactment" of realities, which would view realities as being produced in practices and beliefs. A proper method would be something

Technologies of religion 13

like a "praxiography." But it does not, as Law is quick to remind, follow, then, that there are plural worlds. Plurality entails categorical distinctions. It suggests hard boundaries. It is not a world of "an indefinite number of different and disconnected bodies." It does not imply fragmentation. Instead, a praxiography suggests an overlap and interfering of realities with one another with their relations being "partially co-ordinated," "complex," and "messy" (Law 2004: 61). To think about a "multi-site" methodology would be to think about how sites relate to one another. A methodology grappling with multisited reality must approximate, what he calls, "method assemblage" (2004: 161), which is sensitive to "relations [intersecting] and [resonating] together in unexpected ways" (2004: 156).

Rather appropriate, for this study at least, is the example that Law uses of the method assemblage, which contains overt religious significance – the Quaker prayer meeting. The Quakers, unlike many of their fellow Christians, take the "priesthood of all believers" very seriously. So much so that there is a tradition of unprogrammed worship, wherein a congregation gathers silently until one is moved to speak. According to Law, the silence and the prayer "breaks down" the "everyday habits of selfhood," a sense of self based on hard categorical distinctions, "of being an individual with a distinct and separate identity...with specific and personal goals and plans." The object of the prayer meeting, however, is to tear down these boundaries so as to be "used" by the Spirit, which is "difficult to detect for most of us in the everyday rush of events" (Law 2004: 115).

Thus, the "ethnographic" method deployed here is in large part unrecognizable if viewed through the lens of mainstream social science. It does not aim to offer a systematic portrait of the "lifeworld" of a defined social group, such as in the tradition of urban ethnography or the congregational studies in the sociology of religion. Instead, I follow Christine Hine, who has dubbed her particular bringing-together of STS and multisite ethnography as "almost doing ethnography," or "virtual ethnography" (Hine 2007). This means not only studying technologies in multiple sites, but also exploring how various sites define and inform each other (for instance, analyzing connections between online and offline religious practices without assuming that they are necessarily distinct spheres), and doing so without setting out with a defined idea of technology-use in advance but viewing them *in situ*, that is, as enacted; or, as Alex Wilkie, a sociologist of design, states "the empirical [as] actively constituted out of additions and relations between bodies, objects, practices and words" (Wilkie 2010: 64). The rethinking of the "empirical" as relationally constituted, occasioned by Law, extends also to the manner in which I weave between theory and "data" over the course of this book. Therefore, I tend to vacillate between "ethnographic" observation and theoretical concerns. In some ways, one could say that I have an "empirical" background. Thus, in contrast to having a theoretical thread that weaves a book together like in many social scientific studies, this book addresses various theoretical *problematiques* while referring frequently to Bright Church, one of the largest

14 *Technologies of religion*

multisite churches in the United States, whose use of technology has been widely commented upon within and outside of Christian circles.

"Bright Church" is a pseudonym for one of the largest multisite churches in the United States today in terms of attendance. Its headquarters are located in a Plains state in the south-central US. I have decided to change minor biographical details and provide aliases to interview subjects not so much in order to protect confidentiality and anonymity, as I have obtained consent to use their proper names, but rather, for style and the particular aim of the book. The book is not meant as a detailed study of a singular congregation, as in the community studies of Nancy Ammerman (Ammerman 1987) and Robert Orsi (Orsi 2002). While I use Bright Church, as an example, I did not wish to portray the present study in the same light. These studies are comprised of "thick descriptions" of the social dynamics among religious folk, offering a nearly complete picture of the lifeworld of individuals in small communities of faith. The present study is not that. While it dabbles in ethnography and even auto-ethnography, it does not adhere to the conventions of ethnographic studies, as traditionally understood. I do so because I see this work, primarily, as a work of critical social theory.

And thus, the book begins with chapter 1, by delving deeper into themes already mentioned, regarding the conceptualization of religion and technology within the broader debates around modernity and secularism. I analyze the Weberian concept of "disenchantment" beyond the epistemological conflict narrative usually attributed to it by social science and, instead, argue that that disenchantment not only describes rationalization and intellectualization but actually amounts to a revolution in the foundational intellectual layout of modernity. By revisiting disenchantment, I attempt to move the discussions of religion and technology away from epistemological matters, which too often focus on their incommensurability in the context of modernity, toward ontological concerns, where religion and technology, I argue, are not only compatible but often rooted in the same aim.

Chapter 2 continues with this thread by tracing the ontological aspects that are inherent in major theoretical studies of religion and technology, analyzing the writings of Peter Berger, Mircea Eliade, Heidegger, and Don Ihde. Drawing on a certain reading of them, I pose the thesis that the recent convergence of religion and technology today is due to their respective cosmogonic, or "world-building," and ontologically *creative* qualities. This chapter, therefore, functions to lay the foundation for the underlying argument for the following two chapters – chapters 3 and 4 – which is that the religious use of digital technologies takes on "spherical" – that is, environmental or architectural – qualities, to use the language of philosopher Peter Sloterdijk.

Hence, chapters 3 and 4 can be seen as companions. They both take as points of departure, the example of Bright Church, and take on different aspects of Bright Church's interaction with digital technology and digital culture. Chapter 3 focuses on spatiality, analyzing the techno-physical aspects of Bright Church's spaces of worship. Consisting of ethnographic analysis of the worship experience (and the digital technologies that facilitate it) as well as the Christian trade literature of technology, it centers on how digital technologies construct an "atmosphere," imparting an affective connection and bonding with the pastor and other worshipers who are in distant locations through a formation of an (atmo)sphere. It proposes that the environment of the technologized worship space hints at a shift toward "liturgical aesthetics," which emphasizes images, embodiment, and sensations.

Chapter 4 addresses communality, analyzing the informational architecture of Bright Church's activities online, which include online worship, social media, and microsites, and how they reproduce and remediate the traditional functions of the church lobby (e.g. fellowship) and of the sanctuary (e.g. worship). Taking on these specific technical aspects of Bright Church's online activities, the chapter suggests that the logic of religious communality has moved from "membership" to "network," rewriting the definitions of participation and ritual, questioning the location of the sacred, which, as the chapter suggests, is clearly no longer in the church.

Chapter 5 picks up on some of the theoretical implications of the previous chapter regarding the "location of the sacred" but takes it in a slightly different, and broader direction. It asks whether the sacred can be found in contemporary capitalism, specifically consumer culture. Stringing together themes addressed in previous chapters regarding the increasingly digital and social contours of religious life today, in this chapter I bring them to bear on whether we are entering a "post-secular" age, as many theorists have suggested, and what that may mean in terms of contemporary capitalism.

In the final chapter, I offer some concluding thoughts on whether we can see the developments covered over the course of the book as a return of the sacred.

1 Disenchantment revisited

Formations of the "secular" and "religious" in the technological discourse of modernity

> One of the most damaging ideas that has swept the social sciences and humanities has been the idea of a disenchanting modernity.
>
> (Nigel Thrift 2007: 65)

Introduction

As alluded to in the Introduction, in the confines of contemporary academic discourse, but also in the greater landscape of public debate, a peculiar sense of wonderment is often produced when the basic tenets and assumptions of modernity, its "metaphysics" as Heidegger once said, are challenged. It is a bizarre dance, an exercise in self-deception to a certain extent. What I mean is that many people, not just scholars, understand "modernity," that troubling word which we have inherited, to be something to the tune of what Anthony Giddens has called "living in a *post*-traditional world" (Beck *et al.* 1994, emphasis added), that is, *beyond* tradition. But when they attain visibility, the remnants of so-called traditional life put the modern into sharp relief. A feigning of curiosity results, taking on a distinctly ethnographic flavor. It is as if after the onset of modernity (whenever this may be – sixteenth century and beyond according to many accounts), "the traditional," an ever more elusive term, was wiped away completely.

This bewilderment is nowhere exemplified better than when the technological aspects of contemporary life are juxtaposed with leftover phenomena of our supposedly traditional past, especially religion. Take, for instance, a photograph made popular by the columnist Thomas Friedman. There stands an orthodox Jewish man pressing a mobile phone against the Wailing Wall in Jerusalem. The caption reads: "Shimon Biton places his cellular phone up to the Western Wall so a relative in France can say a prayer at the holy site." The book that made this photo popular, *The Lexus and the Olive Tree*, is one which pits two overarching social forces against one another in the era of globalization. There is modernization, on the one hand, symbolized by the Lexus, and tradition, on the other, symbolized by the olive tree:

> half the world seemed to be emerging from the Cold War intent on building a better Lexus, dedicated to modernizing, streamlining and

privatizing their economies in order to thrive in the system of globalization. And half of the world – sometimes half of the same country, sometimes half the same person – was still caught up in the fight over who owns which olive tree. Olive trees ... represent everything that roots us, anchors us, identifies us and locates us in this world – whether it be belonging to a family, a community, a tribe, a nation, a religion, or, most of all, a place called home. Olive trees are what give us the warmth of family, the joy of individuality, the intimacy of personal rituals, the depth of private relationships, as well as the confidence and security to reach out and encounter others.

(Friedman 2000: 31)

The photo's semiotic contradiction acts as visual leitmotif for the story that Friedman wishes to tell. The man holding the mobile is not just Jewish, but orthodox. He is clad in the traditional clothing of a particular strand of ultra-Orthodox Judaism, black hat and coat; he is donned with thick, curled sideburns, called *payots*, and a beard. All of these details do the work of conveying to the audience that this man is not simply a man of faith but devout. He is at one of the holiest sites of the Abrahamic religions praying with not exactly the most holy of objects, a cellular phone. It is this juxtaposition of the ancient (even Biblical) and the modern, which has given this particular photograph such poignancy. This type of response represents a "false norm" (Habermas 1985), which in this instance is really a false dichotomy between "religion" (the olive tree) and "technology," the latter serving as a proxy for "modernity" (the Lexus). The photograph becomes the perfect illustrative vehicle for Friedman's argument in the book, which is that, at various times, "the Lexus *and* the olive tree" turns into the Lexus *versus* the olive tree.

The thinking exhibited in Friedman's dichotomous thematization of globalization is none other than, I would argue, a popularized secularization theory for the global age, which, after Jeremy Stolow, I call the "myth of modernization."

This is the myth which credits modern media – beginning with the printing press – with a key role in the world-historical disembedding of religion from public life, and its relocation within the private walls of bourgeois domesticity, or deeper still, the interior silent universe of individual readers and their infinitely replicable activities of decoding texts. For some, this is a tale about loss of meaning and moral crisis that comes with the dematerialization of palpable structures of religious authority. For others, it is a heroic story about the empowerment of social groups to challenge the repressive apparatuses of Church and Court ... This meta-narrative is structured around the assumption that the mere expansion of modern communication technologies is somehow commensurate with a dissolution of religious authority and a fragmentation of its markers of affiliations and identity.

(Stolow 2005: 122)

18 *Disenchantment revisited*

From Stolow, we can say that lodged in the concept of secular modernity is an implicit theory of media and technology, one that equates not only their internal logic as commensurate with the *ratio* of formal rationality but also their proliferation and wide use as indicative of the decline of tradition, including religion.

Secularization theory, at least in its recent sociological articulation, maintains that secularization "has been a phenomenon concomitant with modernization," as Bryan Wilson, one of its chief proponents, puts it (Wilson 1998: 52). Of the three areas that he argues are the core concerns of the secularization thesis – authority, knowledge, and rationality, it is the "powerful imprint" of the changing nature of the second – knowledge – that he claims, "no aspect of social change has escaped." He points specifically to the role of science and technology in "[rendering] otiose supernaturalist dogmas and theological speculations about the nature of life and creation. Religionists have been entirely displaced in the interpretation of such matters, their earlier theories and prescriptions have not only lost their cogency but have been shown to be hollow, ignorant and false" (Wilson 1998: 50). As Talal Asad notes, "'the secular' [in the discourse of modernity] presents itself as the ground from which theological discourse was generated (as a form of false consciousness) and from which it gradually emancipated itself in its march to freedom" (Asad 2003: 192). Thus, we can say Friedman basically adopts this under-standing, that is, of modernization as *rationalization*, which is, in turn, set in opposition to non-rational, traditional thinking, which amounts to, in the Marxist parlance used sardonically by Asad, "false consciousness."

But it must be said that Friedman is not alone when it comes to the cheap adoption of secularization theory. His is not a simple case of a journalist wading into academic waters, hacking away complexity and nuance along the way. As sociologists John Evans and Michael Evans note, a similar logic exists in academic studies of religion and science, sociology among them. They identify an "epistemological conflict narrative," which they write is "an assumption ... built into the history of Western academic thought" (Evans and Evans 2008: 87). Put simply, this narrative views the conflict between religion and science as "over competing truth about the world" (Evans and Evans 2008: 88). In their critical unearthing of it in a variety of scholarly lit-eratures, they make note of the wide reach of the influence of Weber, espe-cially the famed notion of "disenchantment." Specifically, in secularization theory, they diagnose a specific form of the epistemological conflict narrative, which they describe as "symbolic." The *symbolic* epistemological conflict narrative sees as parallel the growth of a modern technoscientific rationality with secularity. "Mysterious forces and powers have been replaced by the calculation and technical means embodied in modern science," they write (Evans and Evans 2008: 91), leaving "religion" and, more specifically, reli-gious thinking marginalized. Evans and Evans show that this conflict narrative places "religion" and "science" in a deadlock. They rightly point out that it renders religion and technoscience as mere ways of "knowing about the

Disenchantment revisited 19

world" and nothing else.[1] The conflict narrative makes religion only "symbolic" not material. It is rendered a category of thought and stripped of any other kind of influence or action. The conflict narrative maintains a view of religion as well as science and technology as largely fighting over Truth, which in this instance is singular and uncomplicated. It follows then that scholarly literature which assumes the logic of conflict in disenchantment understands "the secular" to also then simply be a "mindset." *Pace* epistemological conflict, the story of disenchantment (and hence secularization and modernization), is one wherein a set of ideas (traditional/religious) replaces another (modern/rational).

This becomes rather clear not only in secularization theory and studies of religion but also in modernity theory, where the correlation of modernity with technology (Thompson 1995) is nearly unquestionable. Technology has not only "made modernity possible," as Philip Brey writes, but it is also "a creation of modernity" (Brey 2004: 33). The institutions and culture of modernity are not merely "shaped or influenced by technology," they are also "constituted by it" (Brey 2004: 54). But as the critical theorist of technology Andrew Feenberg notes, modernity theory depends on a specific definition of rationalization as a "spontaneous consequence of the pursuit of efficiency once customary and ideological obstructions are removed" (Feenberg 2010: 134–135). This definition of rationalization reflects the influence of Weber, Feenberg contends, specifically, the concept of "bureaucratic rationality," which sees rationalization as becoming efficient through the parsing out, or "disaggregation" of various spheres. For instance, at the level of social structures, "the state, the market, religion, law, art, science, technology" become "distinct social domains with their own logic and institutional identity" (Feenberg 2010: 136). Hence, modernization-*qua*-rationalization-*qua*-differentiation relies upon a view of technological rationality as streamlining, through the eradication of customs and ideologies in order to create distinct, rule-following "bureaus" or offices. Scientific-technological rationality, in Weber's thinking, purifies all that it encounters from "*religious…*elements" (Feenberg 2010: 136, emphasis added). But these "religious elements" are clearly meant to refer to superstition and what Asad earlier calls "theological discourse." Scientific-technological rationality does not necessarily remove ritual *per se* but replaces its source, its reason. Hence, as Feenberg notes, in modernity theory one also finds an emphasis on the rationality of technology (viz. efficiency), not necessarily the dynamics of technology itself. Therefore, analysis of the modernizing effect of technology remains at the level of thought. Technology loses its material weight.

In this chapter, I aim to analyze the Weberian concept of "disenchantment" beyond the epistemological conflict narrative by exploring its ontological aspects. I argue that that disenchantment is not merely just another term for rationalization and intellectualization but a descriptor for a revolution in the traditional layout of the relations between humans, nature, and God, or what I call "onto-cosmology." Unlike its traditional antecedent, the modern world

20 *Disenchantment revisited*

viewed "the human" as its fulcrum, with its operative key words being Progress and history. Disenchantment, in the reading that I'm offering here, is not simply intellectual but environmental. I proceed in three steps: First, I present an "interpretive genealogy" of technological rationality in discourses about modernity, and suggest that even while they contain a Weberian substrate, they nevertheless display an internal conflict, especially in how they formulate "religion," "secular," and "technology." More strongly, I argue that the lack of conceptual consistency in the invocation of these terms is a symptom of a deeper unresolved ontological (or, onto-cosmological) tension in modern thought. This tension revolves around the relational status of the figures of "the human," "nature," and "God." I use these terms not as definitions of extant, transhistorical realities but as concepts that are forged and maintained continuously. Following Bruno Latour, I use these terms as markers of an ontological shift specific to modernity that allows us to hone in the notion of disenchantment. Second, after having established this ontological aporia, I offer a rereading of Weber's original concept of disenchantment, drawing from media scholar Jeremy Stolow and political scientist Gilbert Germain, and suggest that when looked at more closely, religion and technology occupy similar "onto-cosmological" positions vis-à-vis nature, as they are both attempts to effect control over it. Lastly, I tease out some of the implications of this argument for the understanding of religion and technology in contemporary times.

The permutations of "technological rationality" in the discourse of modernity

In this section, I demonstrate a brief "interpretive genealogy" of "technical rationality" in modernity discourses. Due to constraints of time and space, I cannot claim to offer an exhaustive critical assessment of technology-informed works on modernity but, following Aronowitz (1993), I instead provide a "reading" of certain influential thinkers and present conceptual clarifications while highlighting a cluster of relevant aspects of their work. As Aronowitz notes, an "interpretive genealogy" differs from other approaches because "the object" is not taken as given, with a "definite history, cast of characters and well-defined mode of intellectual interventions within a fairly well established field of academic knowledge" (Aronowitz 1993: 7). It allows for the study of tendencies, "to tease out what is left unsaid" (Aronowitz 1993: 8). I do so here to point out not only the inconsistency in the way that not only "technology" is deployed but also how "rationalization" is understood, is symptomatic of a deeper unresolved ontological (or, onto-cosmological) conflict.

More to the point, in the genealogy I sketch below, the effects of technology and the aspects of technological rationality are defined in a rather contrasting manner in spite of the clear influence of Weber. In what I label "modernity as massification," technology becomes a disindividualizing force, effectively "mechanizing" humans. The language used by these authors suggests that technology is not only a modernizing force but also one that reduces or takes away some vague human spiritual essence. In contrast, "modernity as technological atomization" formulates technology as an isolating force, separating humans from one another, leaving them with a communality deficit. Thus, on the one hand, technology and modernity come together to produce mass conformity, while on the other, they come together resulting in anomie.

The theme of "mass" is particularly evident in a strain of existential philosophy associated with Karl Jaspers and Gabriel Marcel. What is significant about their work is not only the use of theological language, but the shared diagnosis of modernity: the technological mechanization of individual personality. Whereas traditional times allowed for "man" [sic] to have a stable knowledge of himself in relation to the world, modernity has ripped the rug from underneath him, throwing him into a seemingly never-ending Heraclitean flux of movement, a consequence of "despiritualization." Or, as Marcel puts it, "Man is in his death-throes" (Marcel 1962: 13–14). Technological modernity, in this line of thinking, is always degrading to the human spirit. But for these thinkers, the "spirit" they speak of is always an individual one. In terms that prefigure the Frankfurt School, especially Marcuse (Marcuse 2002), Marcel argues that "man becomes dependent on gadgets whose smooth functioning assures him a tolerable life at the material level, the more estranged he becomes from an awareness of his inner reality" (Marcel 1962: 55), calling this "technical man" (Marcel 1962: 75). But this "new man," as he alternatively puts it, suffers from a spiritual – a word favored by both him and Jaspers – defect: "he loses touch with himself" (Marcel 1962: 18). Hence, the "uprooting of man" by "advanced technique" (Jaspers 1957: 21) is not only a metaphor of detachment but also, most critically, of its "[absorption] into the social," leading to a "danger to man's selfhood" (Jaspers 1957: 47). In sum, the individual is no longer a self but rather a "function." Jacques Ellul describes the unstoppable, amoeba-like integrative-function of technique technology in a similar manner when he writes, "Technique attacks man, impairs the sources of his vitality, and takes away his mystery" (Ellul 1964: 413).

The idea that modernity with its complex of techniques, characterized by their impersonal bureaucratic nature, has chipped away at the metaphysics of human beings through the process of rationalization is clearly reminiscent of Weber. Technology's cold and calculating character undermines the enchanted mystery of humanity's Being, his individuality.

A nearly opposite tact comes from the philosopher Albert Borgmann (2003). For him, technology does not provide enough communality, leaving the individual atomized in an anomic state. The information technologies of today are the exemplars of what have been the worst tendencies of technological rationality since the end of World War II; they intensify the "drift away from public and civic engagement" thanks to an overdevelopment of convenience after which "all the world is at one's call and beckon, and hence to venture out into the world begins to feel like a waste and a pain" (Borgmann 2003: 77). Invoking Robert Putnam, Borgmann argues that contemporary

22 *Disenchantment revisited*

technologies have exacerbated the fragmentation and atomization of society. This is most clear, he suggests, in the rewriting of the public/private distinctions in advanced industrial societies. The public sphere, in his words, "has become both hypertrophied and atrophied," while the private sphere has become utterly closed off. "As public space has been taken over by instrumentality (i.e., production and administration)," he writes, "finality (i.e., consumption) has passed into the private realm" (Borgmann 2003: 40).

What we have then is a culture wherein legitimate forms of "communal celebration" are extremely rare. Borgmann bemoans the televising of public sporting events such as the Olympics, for instance, because he believes that the mediation of such creates social distance and commodifies the collective experience one would get if he or she were to be there in person. Technology, in this case television, "makes genuine public celebration impossible because the public realm is production, not celebration, and though the private realm is for leisure, leisure is now commodious consumption, not festive engagement" (Borgmann 2003: 46). Thus, technology has left us with a "semblance of the public" rooted in "indifference and disengagement" (Borgmann 2003: 50).

Although both versions of "the myth of social modernization" bear the Weberian substrate of increasing technological disenchantment of the human being, a technological modernity that chips away at a certain metaphysics of the human, there is a clear difference in the understanding of the nature of this dynamic. In the discourse of technological rationality as massification, technologies dis-individualize, and thus de-spiritualize, the human. For Jaspers, technique is "despiritualizing." For Marcel, more dramatically, the effect of technology on humanity is "degrading." While no overt theological themes are addressed by these authors, it is clear that there is an extant metaphysics of the human in their discussions. The human takes on a privileged status to the point where the object of the disenchanting force of technological modernity is *not* God but the human. The principal cause for alarm is not that God is in "death throes" but that the human is. What we have, in effect, is an apotheosis effect.

On the other hand, in the discourse-of-technological-rationality-as-atomization camp, technologies intensify individualization. The view of technology as atomization is quite simply that technologies are by nature divisive, allowing for individuals to be sprawled out, distant from one another and without opportunities to forge communal bonds, which occur mostly through collective ritual. The worry is not that individuals will be overrun by technological conformity, but that there is a deficit of such, as a result of which they will become isolated.

The former narrative bears traces of the Frankfurt School and Reich, while the latter echoes communitarian thinkers such as Rawls (1985, 1987) and Taylor (2003).

So, while we can say, following Evans and Evans as well as Feenberg, that the influence of Weber looms large in the propagation of the "myth of social modernization" in studies of secularization, modernity, and technology, it seems that there is, within theoretical discourses that take Weber as their base, a fundamental disagreement in the effect of modernizing technologies on the human being. To investigate this incongruity, we must investigate Weber's idea of "disenchantment" itself.

Disenchantment beyond rationalization

Weber's essay "Science as a Vocation" (1918) contains the most sustained discussion of the concept of disenchantment. Rather interestingly, he aims to present a methodological argument, largely derived from Kant, about what he calls the "cultural sciences." Although it is not a stated focus, the themes of religion, science, modernity, and rationalization – present in the entirety of Weber's oeuvre – can be found, and serve as the argumentative "background," providing a context for his insistence on the importance of viewing science as "the calling" of modern humanity. And it might be that because Weber's most prolonged engagement with "disenchantment" comes in an essay about method, that many who cite "Science as a Vocation" do so and simply reproduce the commonplace interpretation of *Entzauberung* as epistemological modernization.

If we look closer, however, "disenchantment" in Weber falls under larger metaprocesses of modernity, namely rationalization and intellectualization. But rationalization and intellectualization do not guarantee the dispersal of scientific knowledge throughout all strata of society. It is something slightly different. There are no longer "mysterious incalculable forces that come into play, but rather that one can, in principle, master all things by calculation" (Weber 1958: 117). In other words, the world is "disenchanted" because there is no longer anything therein that is not available for inquiry. If one wished to look into the mechanics of streetcars, one, conceivably, *could*. It is not taken to be the work of magic.

Honing in on this specific part of Weber's argument, scholars such as Jeremy Stolow (2013) and Gilbert Germain (1993) put forth "demagification" as a more apt translation of *Entzauberung* than "disenchantment." Foregrounding "magic" shifts the issue of science, religion, and modernity towards ontological considerations. Magic, Stolow notes, "is the family of tools, techniques, and understandings of the world," which "is supposedly located within the province of the 'primitive mind': as a parapractical mode of action and a prerational effort to explain causal forces in the universe" (Stolow 2013: 9). Malinowski most famously makes the distinction between magic and science in this manner:

> Science is born of experience, magic made by tradition. Science is guided by reason and corrected by observation, magic, impervious to both, lives in an atmosphere of mysticism. Science is open to all, a common good of the whole community, magic is occult, taught through mysterious initiations, handed on in a hereditary or at least in a very exclusive filiation.

24   Disenchantment revisited

> While science is based on the conception of natural forces, magic springs from the idea of a certain mystic, impersonal power, which is believed in by most primitive peoples.
>
> (Malinowski 1954: 19–20)

Magic is, however, akin to science in the sense that they both arise from "man's confidence that he can dominate nature directly" (Malinowski 1954: 19). Thus, Stolow concludes:

> Magic is the ancestor (illegitimate cousin) of what we moderns call technology. In the larger historical scheme of things, magic is something that was (or ought to have been) superseded by a more sober reliance upon techniques and instruments that "actually do their jobs" and by the advancement of scientific reasoning that "properly" frames knowledge about such work.
>
> (Stolow 2013: 9)

In an enchanted age, Germain summarizes, "the means of control is conditioned by the belief that the natural environment is governed by spiritual forces residing in or beyond the immanent order of nature itself." Therefore, in an enchanted world, "magical means" are used to affect the natural realm – "various rites of appeasement, such as sacrifices, ceremonial dances, and so on" (Germain, 1993: 29). In other words, magic and technology are similar in their ontological positions; they are both attempts "to effect real control over natural processes" (Germain 1993: 29).

What distinguishes a disenchanted world from an enchanted world is not merely the epistemological "opening up" of a world through scientific knowledge but "one in which all domains within society are restructured in accordance with the demands of technical rationality" (Germain 1993: 37). Therefore, we can gather that Weber, when he placed the process of "disenchantment" under the larger umbrella heading of "rationalization," did not mean science as purely theoretical knowledge, delinked from its applied use upon nature (to frame it in Heideggerian terms). What he was really referring to was science as it is translated unto the level of praxis. Thus, he pronounced, "today the routines of everyday life challenge religion" (Weber 1958: 127). This presents us with an alternative to the easy conclusion that relies upon the false dichotomy that characterizes the relationship of religion and science as an *epistemological* end game. It is also an ontological shift. Stolow again:

> Technology thus plays a leading role in some of the most prevalent accounts of modernity as the outcome of the disenchantment of nature and society: a historical process that has turned the world into an inert

cosmos, subject to human powers of detached observation and calculated manipulation.

(Stolow 2013: 12)

Following Germain and Stolow, I am suggesting that disenchantment is not simply an extension of the metaprocesses of rationalization and intellectualization. Disenchantment describes a reconfiguration in the traditional layout of the relations between humans, nature and God, or what I call "onto-cosmology." In the modern world, "the human" has become the fulcrum. The world, and history itself, has come to be measured in human terms. Or, as Marcel Gauchet (1999: 59) puts it, "human actors now [gain] access to the mastery of their collective destiny through the realization of the divine infinite." Instead of a magical-mythical world, we have a human-technological world, magic being replaced by technoscience and myth by humanism.

Re-enchanting nature, re-enchanting technology

Consequently, we must now reckon with the repercussions of this onto-cosmological understanding of disenchantment. If technology replaces magic in terms of what can control and master the cosmos, then nature, God, and the human acquire new meanings as their relational logic has changed. Nature is "desacralized," as "standing-reserve," opened up to technological mastery. "[T]he modern definition of technology thus posits a fundamental divide between human and nonhuman agents," Stolow notes. It is this split that fuels the potential "threat for authentic human experience," including religion (Stolow 2013: 13).

I have been using the terms "nature," "human," and "God," following Bruno Latour, who, for some time, has treated the separation of the human and the nonhuman as his primary theoretical problematic. Under the heading of "the modernist settlement" or "modern constitution," Latour has suggested that "modernity," as it has been largely understood in terms of the Enlightenment – "the invention of humanism," "the emergence of the sciences," "the secularization of society" and "the mechanization of the world" – is wrong. Modernity arises out of an ontological settlement wherein subjects and objects are divided. The former are housed in "society" and the latter housed in "nature" (Latour 1999: 193). The former are humans and the latter are nonhumans. The former have agentive properties while the latter are incapable of action. In terms more in line with social thought:

Modernity is often defined in terms of humanism, either as a way of saluting the birth of "man" or as a way of announcing his death. But this habit itself is modern, because it remains asymmetrical. It overlooks the simultaneous birth of "nonhumanity" – things, or objects, or beasts – and

26 *Disenchantment revisited*

> the equally strange beginning of a crossed-out God, relegated to the sidelines.
>
> (Latour 1993: 13)

In this originary setting of stage, humans, nonhumans, and God share a "conjoined birth" but are separated immediately. "Nature" is then that which houses "nonhumans" and "society" is that which houses humans. God is relegated to the beyond, the transcendent. Each of these is not a static given.

But why? What are the stakes for this "modern constitution"?

There are two interrelated net effects of this ontological layout. On the one hand, there is the achievement of Progress. By identifying, and differentiating, "what objects really are in themselves and what the subjectivity of humans believes them to be, projecting onto them passions, biases and prejudices," modernity is able to congratulate itself for no longer being mired in the confusion of the past (Latour 1999: 199). Part and parcel to that is a guarantee: the guarantee that God does not meddle. "God becomes the crossed-out God of metaphysics," writes Latour. God is kept "from interfering with Natural Law as well as with laws of the Republic" (Latour 1993: 33). And thus, the realm of nature and that of humans both are kept God-free in the modernist settlement. Having an ontological scene with an extant but non-intervening God allows for a situation of what Latour refers to caustically as "invincibility of the moderns" (Latour 1993: 37).

> Solidly grounded in the certainty that humans make their own destiny, the modern man or woman can criticize and unveil, express indignation at and denounce irrational beliefs, the biases of ideologies, and the unjustified domination of the experts who claim to have staked out the limits of action and freedom.
>
> (Latour 1993: 36)

Zooming out a little bit, we can say that Latour provides us with the ontological significance of an environmental reading of disenchantment that Germain set forth. As one would expect, for Latour, the proper reading of disenchantment is precisely its jettisoning. This is because, according to him, we have never truly been modern. The separation of the human and nonhuman was never truly accomplished. The ethos of purification that left nature and society as distinct entities (and relegated God to the sidelines) never reflected what Latour views as the truth of the contemporary situation. As he writes, "the adjective modern does not describe an *increased distance* between society and technology or their alienation, but a deepened *intimacy*, a more intricate mesh, between the two." This is not only the case in "traditional cultures," where, for instance, "the intricate pattern of myths and rites necessary to produce the simplest adze or the simplest pot, [reveal] that a variety of social graces and religious mores were necessary for humans to interact with non-human" but also contemporary "biotechnology, artificial intelligence, microchips, steelmaking, and so on" (Latour 1999: 196). Even Bryan Wilson, the authority on secularization, cedes this point:

> Think only of the significance of techniques in the most intimate areas of human experience and relationship, of birth control, of invitrio [sic] fertilization, of genetic engineering. Or consider the transformed patterns of human intercourse progressively from railways, telephones, aeroplanes, radio, television, computers and the Internet. Recall that men now travel in space, walk on the moon, and, at long-distance, explore other planets.
>
> (Wilson 1998: 50)

This leads us to think about what Weber would think of Latour's argument. If indeed technology has granted ontology to the same degree as humans, then we have a situation that forces a rethinking of the very basis of modernist settlement. Technology, as capable of action, also reflects a "practical metaphysics" (Latour 1999: 287). This means that not only religion, as authentic human experience, in the words of Stolow, but also technology, enchants. Or, as Germain concludes, "we could say that our technological environment has acquired 'magical' qualities."

> What Weber could have chosen to comment on, but tellingly did not, are the potential consequences of living in a world that is both technologically powerful and enigmatic. If he had, he might have come to the conclusion that our disenchanted world is in danger of becoming re-enchanted. Only this time the "gods" would appear not in the form of the supernatural but in the immanent guise of technology itself.
>
> (Germain 1993: 42)

Conclusion

In this chapter, I have problematized the reading of the Weberian concept of disenchantment as "rationalization" and revealed the "inoperativity" (Nancy 1991) of certain categories upon which the idea of "disenchanting modernity" is rooted. I suggested that the proliferation of this reading of Weber has resulted in the overlooking of the ontological effects of secular modernity. By offering an alternative rereading of Weber, I demonstrated that religion and technology take on conceptual definitions that require us to rethink "secularization" and its bases but also the assumptions around the meaning of modernity that lies within it. Moreover, as we are reminded more and more of religion's "technicity" (Campbell 2010), it becomes ever more crucial to consider the "technological" alongside "the religious." Given this, it may be that the ultimate import of Weber's concept of "disenchantment" is not as an explicatory, sociological grand narrative of modernity and secularization but rather as a prompt to reconsider the "givenness" of "the modernist settlement," providing

28 *Disenchantment revisited*

insight into the constitutive place of "the religious" and "the technological" in the constitution of modernity's secular metaphysics.

Note

1 Although their critique of this "epistemological" narrative is a much welcomed objection to the rather simplistic opposition of religion and science that exists in much of the recent sociological scholarship on secularism and modernity, Evans and Evans go on to argue in favor of "social-institutional" analyses of science and religion as a much needed corrective to the dominance of "symbolic" analyses. In other words, they claim that there is too much consideration of religion and science as ideologies in the most neutral sense of that term, as sets of ideas or beliefs at the cost of viewing them as institutions with "competing interests."

2 From cosmos to sphere
"Worlds" across religion and technology

Introduction

The concept of "world," with varying degrees, strikes at the heart of many, if not all, religions. To explain the creation, or origins, of the world is somewhat requisite for what most people would consider a chief function of religion and also science. Specifically, in Western thought, the concept of "world" has had a rather interesting history, receiving much of its importance from a time when the intellectual lines between "religion" and "science" were blurry at best.

Beginning with Galileo and later Newton, "the world" held a distinctly mechanical flavor, what religion and science scholar Ian Barbour calls the "world-as-machine," which meant to view it as "an intricate machine following immutable laws, with every detail precisely predictable" (Barbour 1966: 36). This idea became prevalent in early modern times, a key moment in the intellectual history of the West, in which theology and philosophy were giving way in hegemony to science. As Barbour tells it, the world (in this stage still thought of as the universe) becomes more and more closely aligned with the divine and humans become less and less central to the created order. As a consequence, the Creator's transcendence (and separation from his creation, the world) is intensified. "Newton himself," Barbour writes, "believed that the world-machine was designed by an intelligent creator and expressed his purpose; to later interpreters, impersonal and blind forces appeared to be entirely self-contained, and all sense of meaning and purpose was lost" (Barbour 1966: 36). Thus to find truth in Nature, which for instance was the chief aim of the emergent form of knowledge known as science, as the prior contributions of Galileo had facilitated, was to look for a *mechanism*, something *within* the world that would explain its complexity yet retain some sense of the divine.

Later, Galilean and Newtonian perspectives were successfully combined in the figure of the "Divine Clockmaker" or what is alternatively called the "Watchmaker analogy" in William Paley's *Natural Theology* (Paley 1963).

It was the clock analogy that provided the basic interpretive image of the world as a perfect machine, autonomous and self-sufficient, with natural

30   *From cosmos to sphere*

causes acting in independence of God. "Divine preservation" started as active sustenance, became passive acquiescence, and was then forgotten. Frequent reference was made to God's dominion and governance, but the interpretation given to these terms made them applicable only to the original act of creation.

(Barbour 1966: 42)

A theological consequence of this analogy was that God began to be thought of in terms of Aristotelian First Cause, not a constantly active force in the world. By the beginning of the eighteenth century, Nature, a self-contained machine, is expunged of God altogether, its creator now dwelling, critically, *outside* of the domain of humans. The image of the clockmaker who, once after he creates his product no longer actively intervenes in it, is suggestive of a strategy widely used among early modern philosophers that Barbour calls "God of the gaps." In other words, when early modern philosophy and science begin to take shape and develop their respective fields of knowledge, outside the confines of theology, "God" is utilized to fill in the yet-to-be-explained portions. The analogy of Nature as machine (a clock) and God as Divine Clockmaker, then, reflects not a "deus ex machina" but a "machina ex dei" in early modern philosophy and science. Just as the "deus ex machina" is the means by which ancient Greek drama resolved itself (through the sudden appearance of a god dropped down onto the stage by use of a crane), the "machina ex dei" is the condition of possibility for the Galilean-Newtonian worldview of the seventeenth–eighteenth centuries.

Unlike this "world" of early modern science, philosophy and theology, the notion of "world" explored here draws from an important mention of the origins of the Latin *religio* in the thought of Jacques Derrida. In "Faith and Knowledge" (Derrida 2002), he reminds us of the dual genealogy of the term. On the one hand, *religio* is traced to *relegare*, "to bind back"; on the other, as Cicero does, it is traced to *legere*, "to gather or assemble." The conceptual framework of "worlding" presented here incorporates both genealogical routes. Worlds, as formulated here, are *not* the bounded territories, which "globe" tends to signify, a result of the influence of the order and structure in Aristotelian cosmology. (More on globes below in the discussion of the work of philosopher Jean-Luc Nancy.) Worlds, in our digital age, are no longer neat entities but are modular *milieux, dispositifs*, and assemblages. These new worlds are able to "bind" worlds to other worlds, creating new worlds. They are able to create new "schemata" or "networks" whereby elements from traditionally "separate" ontologies are able to resonate. They are able to de-differentiate, or in a Deleuzian mode, de-territorialize and re-territorialize. They are, in short, recombinant.

Additionally, the concept of "world," and its cognates like "cosmos," has held a prominent place in theoretical studies of religion and technology respectively in the twentieth century. In terms of studies of religion, one could argue that the defining work in the sociology of religion, *The Elementary*

Forms of Religious Life (1912) by Emile Durkheim, was the first to do so by suggesting that religion imparted sacred value upon various objects in the environment of human beings. The dual functions of sanctification and collectivization were evidence for him that God or religion more generally was the apotheosis of the social. Though there is much to be said about some of the other implications of this argument (not a minor one being that Durkheim is clearly outlining a kind of Rousseauian "civil religion" thesis), there is indeed an indication that he is forging a theory of "world," which for him, is rooted in a bonded reverence for the social itself. Durkheim's "world" is a moral world not a physical world such as a globe, but nevertheless it is a world because it entails an ontology and, most evidently, an order.

Here, I wish to develop the thesis that the convergence of religion-technology today is due to their cosmogonic, or "world-building," and ontologically *creative* qualities. However, I contend that a "cosmology" and "ontology" that describes the relation of religion and new media technologies must be viewed as unbounded and networked, and necessarily challenges the restrictiveness of ancient and traditional cosmology, of mostly the Aristotelian variety, that focuses on totality, causality, and order. This I will suggest is occasioned by the dynamic of the current regime of *digital* media technologies, defined by emergence, convergence, creativity, and non-linearity.

This requires a new way of thinking about the concept of "world." In order to attempt a new "world" theory, this chapter will begin with a critical assessment of theories of religion as world-building, focusing particularly on the works of Peter Berger and Mircea Eliade. It will then move on to theories of technology as world-forming, focusing on Martin Heidegger, who is arguably the originator of this argument, and philosopher Don Ihde, a contemporary articulator of a Heideggeran approach to the study of technology. Then, I will move on to a consideration of the work of Jean-Luc Nancy and Peter Sloterdijk. Their recent work, while influenced by Heidegger, moves past his framework of "world" in similar ways, which will be important to the way that "worlds" are conceptualized in the wake of digitization, which will be taken up in the concluding section with the help of the recent work of Mark C. Taylor and William Connolly.

The worlds of religion

In his renowned work, *The Sacred Canopy*, a veritable classic in the sociology of religion, Peter Berger argues that "human religion" is an instance of "human world-building" (Berger 1967: 3). World-building or world-construction is, according to Berger, a basic aspect of human Being. This is because human beings cannot live with ontological insecurity, and therefore must locate themselves within a milieu, a world. "Man," he writes, "must *make* a world for himself. The world-building activity of man, therefore, is not a biologically extraneous phenomenon, but the direct consequence of a man's biological constitution" (Berger 1967: 5).

32 *From cosmos to sphere*

For Berger, the process of locating oneself is essentially dialectical, consisting of three steps: externalization, objectivation, and internalization. Externalization is the "outpouring" of human physical and mental activity. Objectivation is when the products of this activity take on the status of "facticity," that is, as actually existing outside of the human consciousness. Internalization, finally, is the process of "re-appropriating" that objective reality and "transforming it ... from structures of the objective world into structures of the subjective" (Berger 1967: 4). As Berger argues, this is where the human being constructs a world, though not simply for the sake of merely being a creator of one but to also locate herself within it. Thus, the human produces *herself in a world*.

The facticity, or object-ness, of the world is helped along by its collective character. Recalling Durkheim's *conscience collective*, the double-entendre that signifies, in French, both collective *consciousness* and collective *conscience*, Berger suggests that the human collective must not only produce this world but also recognize it. This duality is essential for the eventual internalization of the reality that is objectivated.

> Man's world-building activity is always a *collective* enterprise. Man's internal appropriation of a world must also take place in a *collectivity*. It has by now become a social-scientific platitude to say that it is impossible to be human, in any empirically recognizable form that goes beyond biological observations, except in society. This becomes less of a platitude if one adds that the internalization of a world is dependent on society in the same way, because one is thereby saying that man is incapable of conceiving of his own experience in a comprehensively meaningful way unless such a conception is transmitted to him by means of *social* processes.
>
> (Berger 1967: 16, emphasis added)

Especially of interest here, Berger makes an argument for world-construction as *nomos*, "a meaningful order ... imposed upon the discrete experiences and meanings of individuals" (Berger 1967: 19). The process of world-building, then, is necessarily one that aims to achieve a holistic, systematic explanation of individual experience. There is a tinge of drive theory in Berger. Humans, he states, are "congenitally compelled" to seek order.

A consequence of this will-to-order, as he explains, is that social institutions begin to be endowed with an *ontological* status to the point "where to deny them is to deny being itself – being of the universal order of things, one's own being in this order" (Berger 1967: 24). This ontologization of social institutions he calls "cosmization." As he goes on to explain, when *nomoi* (more than one *nomos*) are objectivated, there "occurs a merging of its meanings with what are considered to be the fundamental meanings inherent in the universe" (Berger 1967: 25). In "traditional" or pre-modern societies, nomos and cosmos maintain this co-extensive relationship in the form of macrocosm/ microcosm, whereby society is a reflection of the natural laws of the universe

From cosmos to sphere 33

on a smaller scale, so to speak. This, he concludes, demonstrates the tendency of humanly constructed *nomoi* to be projected into the universe, the supreme instance of cosmization, producing a cosmology or anthropology, or better yet, an ontology.

Religion, then, is an instance of this kind of cosmization but in a sacred mode. "Sacred" here is seen as bearing "mysterious and awesome power, other than man and yet related to him" (Berger 1967: 34). The cosmos necessarily includes but also transcends the human. While it confronts her as a reality outside of her, the cosmos is crucial in its function as a GPS device of sorts, helping to locate herself through the construction of a meaningful order.

This "locating function" is crucial in the process of world-maintenance. These socially constructed worlds that achieve ontological status – *cosmoses* – are maintained through processes of legitimation. In order to maintain a cosmos, Berger argues that its constructed nature must be hidden as much as possible. People must:

> believe that, in acting out the institutional programs that have been imposed on them, they are but realizing the deepest aspirations of their own being and putting themselves in harmony with the fundamental order of the universe.
>
> (Berger 1967: 33)

Religion fulfills this "task" of world-maintenance quite successfully as it places upon social institutions, and all human phenomena, the validity of ontology, thereby placing constructed institutions within a sacred and cosmic framework. "Cosmization," Berger notes, "implies the identification of this humanly meaningful world with the world as such, the former now being grounded in the latter, reflecting it or being derived from it in its fundamental structures" (Berger 1967: 27).

The sacralization of human *nomoi* has historically had disastrous consequences. One such example is the cosmization that was explicitly used to justify the doctrine known as the Divine Right of Kings. A more contemporary example, as given by Berger, is modern science, which acts as the supreme ontological and cosmological ground today. But even in arguing the ontological aspect of world-construction and maintenance, Berger privileges the epistemological. For instance, he formulates the concept of "plausibility structure," which he describes as the "social base" for the continuing subjective and objective reality of a world (Berger 1967: 45). When articulating the importance of social interaction for the continued recognition and participation in a socially constructed world, Berger argues that this occurs in a shared epistemological, not ontological, plane. Thus, we come to a tension in Berger's theory of "cosmization." Whereas he insists on the ontological disposition of world-construction and world-maintenance, he, in the last analysis, views epistemology as the ultimate ground of cosmos. So when he argues that

34 *From cosmos to sphere*

cosmization is the process by which *nomoi*, the socially constructed institutions of human societies, attain cosmic status, it is merely at the level of ideology. As he himself acknowledges, Berger's theory of cosmization comes directly from Mircea Eliade, especially *The Myth of the Eternal Return: Cosmos and History* (Eliade 1954) and *The Sacred and the Profane: The Nature of Religion* (Eliade 1959).

It is in these works that Eliade outlines his basic definition of religion. All religions involve cosmogony, the act of creating a world, which serves the purpose of differentiating inhabitable space (cosmos) from uninhabitable, indeterminable space (chaos). Cosmos is the space with meaning, whereby objects within are all explained. The relationship between the cosmos and chaos is the spatial expression of the general, theoretical relationship between the sacred and the profane. The profane is not a proper "world." It is a shattered universe of fragments, an amorphous mass.

> The former is the world (more precisely, our world), the cosmos; everything outside it is no longer a cosmos but a sort of "other world," a foreign, chaotic space, peopled by ghosts, demons, foreigners (who are assimilated to demons and the souls of the dead).
>
> (Eliade 1954: 29)

A feature of cosmogony in many archaic societies is the sacred pole, which is erected in a space before inhabitation. The pole acts as an *axis mundi*. It is an ontological establishment of the universe "in a particular place, organizing it, inhabiting it" (Eliade 1954: 34). The pole or the axis is crucial to establishing the sacred space because of its centrality in both symbolic and material terms. As pointed out earlier, Eliade equates sacred space to "world" (more specifically, *our* world) but one that contains an absolute center. That center is the axis or the sacred pole as found in a range of groups such as the Kwakiutl, pre-Christian Celts, and Germans as well as certain tribal groups of Indonesia (Eliade 1954: 35).

A key attribute of sacred space is its capacity to orient the universe and give it form. Consequently, the establishment of the *axis mundi*, and "our world," results in the centering of "our world." The centering is key not only for its representation of spiritual significance (the space and its inhibitors see it as most holy) but also its status as mediator between other cosmic planes. The foundation of the *axis mundi* translates to such a world becoming the basis for an *imago mundi*. As Eliade explains using the example of Palestine:

> Whatever the extent of the territory involved, the cosmos that it represents is always perfect. An entire country (e.g., Palestine), a city (Jerusalem), a sanctuary (the Temple in Jerusalem), all equally well present an *imago mundi* ... It is clear, then, that both the *imago mundi* and the Center are repeated in the inhabited world. Palestine, Jerusalem, and the Temple severally and concurrently represent the image of the universe and the

From cosmos to sphere 35

Center of the World. This multiplicity of centers and this reiteration of the image of the world on smaller and smaller scales constitute one of the specific characteristics of traditional societies.

(Eliade 1954: 42–43)

The reasoning behind the concentric circles of the *imago mundi* for "religious man" was to imagine oneself as living as close to the Center as possible. His home, temple, city and country all become the Center. Therefore, one could say that all of the various spaces that he occupied were sacred; he could "only live in a space opening upward, where the break in plane was symbolically assured and hence communication with the *other world*, the transcendental world, was ritually possible" (Eliade 1954: 44).

As Eliade points out, the development of spatial consecration and inhabitation can not only be found in "traditional societies," by which he clearly meant "primitive," tribal groups, but also in ancient Rome. Though the cross-cultural nature of his argument is questionable as it is clearly Eurocentric, he does provide the insightful example of the Roman *mundus* – "a circular trench divided into four parts; it was at once the image of the cosmos and the paradigmatic model for the human habitation" (Eliade 1954: 44). This quadratic schema of the mundus, Eliade argues, extends from Bali to pre-Christian Germany, the point being that any settling into a territory is a consecration of space. That is to say, any form of inhabitation of space for religious persons is always of a sacred one, which contains the cosmogonic moment – the founding of a world.

[T]he experience of sacred space makes possible the "founding of the world": where the sacred manifests itself in space, *the real unveils itself*, the world comes into existence ... Hence the manifestation of the sacred in space has a cosmological valence; every spatial hierophany or consecration of a space is equivalent to a cosmogony.

(Eliade 1954: 63–64)

In other words, the world inhabited by religious people *must* be sacred because their very being itself is tied directly to the sanctity of the cosmos itself. Religious people display an "ontological thirst," in the attempt to align individual and collective existence with the universe. As Eliade calls it, this is "the anthropo-cosmic" nature of religious life, where "being" and the sacred are the same. "[T]he most elementary religion is," Eliade writes, "above all, an ontology" (Eliade 1954: 210).

Although Eliade insists upon the "there-ness" and facticity of the sacred for the religious person, unlike Berger, even going so far as to suggest that "the manifestation of the sacred ontologically founds the world" (Eliade 1954: 21), he nevertheless maintains a Platonic dualism between the realm of ideas and the realm of the real in his articulation of religion as ontology. Just as in Plato, the cosmos remains at a level beyond the human, for it to draw from

36 *From cosmos to sphere*

and imitate and repeat. In the case of cosmogony, the world-construction ritual of sanctifying inhabitable space can be explained as repetition of the originary Creation of the World. For Eliade, cosmogony is not only hierophany – the revelation of not only a world but also an "absolute reality." Yet, he maintains that this process is *mediated* by the constitution of an absolute center, the *axis mundi*, which takes form in holy sites, such as a temple, basilica or cathedral. The *axis mundi* is, Eliade argues, a means of communication, an opening, a break from one cosmic region to another. The "world" or cosmos then is made real by its adherence to a mythical "archetype" that in turn opens up the connection between it and the cosmos. So while he does not relegate the religious to the realm of ideas, Eliade nonetheless retains a privileging of the archetype (an idea or perhaps memory) over the sacred cosmos.

Berger and Eliade share two fundamental characteristics in their formulations of religious worlding. First, "cosmos" is an ideological construct that does not have material consequence. And, second, ontology or Being is strictly an effect of knowledge. These conclusions coincide with critiques of Berger leveled by British theologian John Milbank. As already mentioned, Milbank charges the American tradition sociology of religion, which includes Parsons, Berger, Luckmann, and Bellah, of "policing the sublime," effectively relegating religion to the epiphenomenal. Milbank turns the tables on sociology by arguing that the category of the "social" emerges out of a secularist project whereby "religion" becomes an object of sociological knowledge to "cope" with it, and thus subjecting it to disciplinary (in both senses) analysis. (This, of course, is a clever upturning of Durkheim's argument that God is the apotheosis of the social.) Thus, he goes on to argue, religion becomes equated to the Kantian sublime (Milbank 1990: 104).

Berger, Milbank argues, is guilty of this as he represents "the sacred canopy" as a kind of ideological defense mechanism used by societies to explain the prevailing social norms and institutions. As the Greeks used Prometheus and Persephone to intellectually account for the presence of fire and the seasonal change, the sacred canopy – religion – is functionally mythology, a set of ideas and stories that take on the status of social knowledge. As Milbank calls it, Berger's theory of religion is a theory of "general occlusion" (Milbank 1990: 137).

Certainly, then, Milbank confirms what was earlier proposed about Berger's conceptualization of "worlds." They are not much more than worlds of ideas. Berger here reveals his functionalism and mentalism. Religion is "useful for imagining and representing this invisible 'whole' and also for temporarily 'storing up' energies in an 'ideal' realm, which can later be put to 'real social use'" (Milbank 1990: 109). Milbank's critique against Berger is, in sum, that "religion," as he and sociology generally defines it, lacks any kind of ontological substance. This can be extended, though to a lesser degree, to Eliade as well. Although he makes a stronger case for the ontological grounds of "worlding" in that he does not treat religion as epiphenomenal, he nevertheless privileges the realm of ideas. "World", for either of them, if not wholly, is largely ideational.

The worlds of technologies

In two well-known essays, "The Age of the World Picture" (1950) and "The Question Concerning Technology" (1954), Martin Heidegger outlines one of the most influential philosophical approaches to technology in the twentieth century, which Don Ihde, a contemporary philosopher of technology influenced by him, calls the "nonnetural" view (Ihde 1983: 60). Ihde describes it in this way because Heidegger explicitly rejects what is still perhaps the commonsense ("instrumental" or "anthropological") view of technology – as mere tool, which views it as simply a passive means to a human end. The philosopher of technology Andrew Feenberg calls this the "substantive" theory of technology, suggesting that it sees technology as an autonomous cultural force that reconstitutes the relationship of the human to the world, overriding prior value-systems and other areas of social life. But however it is called, technology, in this view, is an actor. As Feenberg describes it, "technology is not simply a means but has become an *environment* and a way of life" (Feenberg 2002: 8, emphasis added).

Within Heidegger's philosophy of technology is an implicit periodization. For him, modern, that is to say, mechanical technologies, do something quite particular, which, in turn, requires a modern philosophy of technology. Modern technologies facilitate *poiesis* and *aletheia*. In the Greek, *poiesis* stands for "to make" or "to create" and *aletheia* "to reveal or make evident," which together form the Heideggerian concept of "presencing." This, he argues, is one of the chief tasks of technology. For him, *poiesis* does not simply signify creation but something particular – "bringing-forth" (Heidegger 1977: 10). As an example, Heidegger offers up another Greek term, *physis*, which usually refers to nature and its machinations – arguably an ancient precursor to what in the Middle Ages and later was referred to as "natural law." Heidegger suggests that *physis* is *poiesis* in the highest sense. "For what presences by means of *physis* has the bursting open belonging to bringing-forth, e.g., the bursting of a blossom into bloom, in itself" (Heidegger 1977: 10). While *poiesis* is equated to "bringing-forth," *aletheia* is equated to what Heidegger calls "unconcealment." As he notes, *techne*, or "craft," has been linked etymologically with *episteme*, both referring to knowledge, in the most general sense. Unconcealment, then, is a kind of *presencing* that "reveals whatever does not bring itself forth and does not yet lie here before us, whatever can look and turn out now one way and now another" (Heidegger 1977: 13). In fact, one could think of *aletheia* similarly to *poiesis*, but with the latter concept containing an element of sui generis.

But the revealing of presencing is not simply a bringing-forth of something that already exists. Something is being *produced*. Unconcealment, then, has a particular character, which Heidegger calls "challenging." Modern technologies "challenge" nature by demanding of it energy to be extracted and stored. Nature, therefore, is brought-forth and revealed as a "standing-reserve" of energy. Modern technologies "enframe" nature within a particular mode of ordering or systematicity.

38   *From cosmos to sphere*

> Enframing is the gathering together that belongs to that setting-upon which sets upon man and puts him in position to reveal the real, in the mode of ordering, as standing-reserve ... Enframing, as a challenging-forth into ordering, sends into a way of revealing. Enframing is an ordaining of destining, as is every way of revealing. Bringing-forth, *poiesis*, is also a destining in this sense.
>
> (Heidegger 1977: 24)

It is "enframing" that is demonstrative of world-forming. The view of nature, as standing-reserve, is not *a priori*; it is a product of the process of "enframing" of technology. Technologies provide a dominant picture of the world, or "world picture" (*Weltbild*).

In modern times, Heidegger suggests, science and technology have "pictured" the world in a particular way.

> One of the essential phenomena of the modern age is its science. A phenomenon of no less importance is machine technology. We must not, however, misinterpret that technology as the mere application of modern mathematical physical science to praxis. Machine technology is itself an autonomous transformation of praxis, a type of transformation wherein praxis first demands the employment of mathematical physical science. Machine technology remains up to now the most visible out-growth of the essence of modern technology, which is identical with the essence of modern metaphysics.
>
> (Heidegger 1977: 116)

For Heidegger, the world picture is always "the ground." By this he means that "world" is not simply a denotation of a certain "scenic" space, a usage which the social sciences more generally are guilty of – i.e., the social world, the psychic world, etc. But for Heidegger, to call something a "world" is to identify a process of binding and cohesion; it is normative, prescriptive. "Picture" refers to its systematicity, like when we say, "we get the picture." We mean that we get the entire picture. So, "world" here refers to something "in its entirety" (Heidegger 1977: 129) and "set in place" (*gestelt*) (Heidegger 1977: 127), like the terms "cosmos," "history," and "nature." As Heidegger explains:

> We mean by it [world picture] itself, the world as such, what is, in its entirety, just as it is normative and binding for us...Where the world becomes picture, what is, in its entirety, is juxtaposed as that for which man is prepared and which, correspondingly, he therefore intends to bring before himself and have before himself, and consequently intends in a decisive sense to set in place before himself. Hence world picture, when understood essentially, does not mean a picture of the world but the world conceived and grasped as picture.
>
> (Heidegger 1977: 129)

From cosmos to sphere 39

"Picture," then, is a signifier of systematicity, a kind of logic that Heidegger suggests is the driving force behind science and technology. A picture that consists of the "entirety" of the world, that is, the world picture, is illustrative of "setting in place" or a modality of representation, signifying the way in which Being is always actualized through representedness, a specific type of representation that privileges presence in the modern age.

> To represent (*vor-stellen*) means to bring what is present at hand (*das Vorhandene*) before oneself as something standing over against, to relate it to oneself, to the one representing it, and to force it back into this relationship to oneself as the normative realm.
>
> (Heidegger 1977: 131)

Therefore, we can summarize Heidegger with the point that the modern world picture is an image "structured" and ordered by technologies, which of course affect how humans view themselves in relation to the world. Heidegger gives two modern examples – the airplane ("the annihilation of great distances") and radio (Heidegger 1977: 135). Planes and radio are two modes of a *dispositif* of technologies that influence everyday understandings of space (distance) and time (simultaneity) that have receded into the ontological "background" of many people today. They are deeply embedded in the "plausibility structure," to use Berger's terminology, of the contemporary world.

Whereas Heidegger uses "world," Ihde uses the more phenomenologically orthodox "lifeworld." Lifeworld, according to Ihde, is the multidimensional structure of experience (Ihde 1990). It is the environment or the milieu in which humans situate themselves. Hence, to say that technologies construct lifeworlds is to suggest that they "[supply] the dominant basis for an understanding both of the world and ourselves" (Ihde 1983: 10). This is so because technologies are inextricably linked to the humanness of humans, as Bernard Stiegler, and Andre Leroi-Gourhan before him, have argued (Stiegler 1998). Certainly, as Ihde suggests, technologies are perhaps the first expression of *praxis*, which "grounds the relationship between humans and their world. Now when this argument is applied to technology, not only can technology be seen to be important, and in a few cases even central, but it is related to the fundamental dimensions of human life itself" (Ihde 1983: 10).

As a phenomenologist, Ihde views the self as "neither self-contained nor separated from a context, a field, a world," mirroring Heidegger's concept of "throwness" (*Geworfenheit*) (Ihde 1983: 14). Ihde carries on the capsizing of the subject–object separation that Heidegger initiated by suggesting that the lifeworld of technology uncovers the "relativistic ontology of human experience" (Ihde 1990: 23). Taking seriously the ontological implications of Heidegger's questioning of the worldhood of the world, Ihde suggests that a relativistic ontology is one that takes the self and the world as located and constituted through a relation. They are not treated as pre-existing entities.

40 *From cosmos to sphere*

The relationality of human-world relationships is claimed by phenomenologists to be an ontological feature of all knowledge, all experience. Negatively, it would be claimed that there is no way to "get out of" this relativistic situation, and any claim to the contrary can be shown to be either naïve or misguided.

(Ihde 1990: 26)

Ihde's conceptualization of the technology and the lifeworld focuses on a particular definition of experience – perception, of which he offers two types.

What is usually taken as sensory perception (what is immediate and focused bodily in actual seeing, hearing, etc.), I shall call microperception. But there is also what might be called a cultural, or hermeneutic, perception, which I shall call macroperception. Both belong equally to the lifeworld. And both dimensions of perception are closely linked and intertwined. There is no microperception (sensory-bodily) without its location within a field of microperception and no macroperception without its micropercetual foci.

(Ihde 1990: 29)

Ihde's argument suggests that technology affects the very vision or perception of the phenomenological subject, echoing the Heideggerian rejection of the anthropocentric view of technology as instrument. There is no such thing as "innocent" or unmediated perception; all perception is "technologically embodied" (Ihde 1983: 44), just as there is no "innocent" or value-free world, but always a "pictured" one.

According to Ihde, when technologies are used to "enhance" perception, such as the case for optical technologies, the perceptual sense, vision in this case, is transformed, as the technological object no longer takes the "position of mediation" but rather withdraws into the seer.

The very first time I put on my glasses, I see the now-corrected world. The adjustments I have to make are not usually focal irritations but fringe ones (such as the adjustment of backglare and the slight changes in spatial motility). But once learned, the embodiment relation can be more precisely described as one in which the technology becomes maximally "transparent." It is, as it were, taken into my own perceptual-bodily self experience thus:

(I-glasses)-world

My glasses become part of the way I ordinarily experience my surroundings; they "withdraw" and are barely noticed, if at all. I have then actively embodied the technics of vision. Technics is the symbiosis of artifact and user within a human action.

(Ihde 2004: 138)

From cosmos to sphere 41

This extended experiential description of the relationship of the phenomenological subject, eyeglasses, and the world demonstrates the principle of embodiment that is characteristic of the relationship between the "user" and technology. The glasses do not impose greatly on the seer. It "withdraws." Ihde notes this withdrawal through the parenthesis. The seer in that instance embodies the technics, which in turn, constitutes a technological lifeworld. Another illustrative example he provides is that of driving a car.

> One experiences the road and surroundings *through* driving the car, and motion is the focal activity…One embodies the car, too, in such activities as parallel parking: when well embodied, one feels rather than sees the distance between car and curb – one's bodily sense is "extended" to the parameters of the driver-car "body." And although these embodiment relations entail larger, more complex artifacts and entail a somewhat longer, more complex learning process, the bodily tacit knowledge that is acquired is perceptual-bodily.
>
> (Ihde 2004: 139)

But the significance of technological embodiment is not limited to the level of the bodily-perceptual. As Ihde notes, technologies affect the "entire gestalt." Using the example of the telescope, he writes, "[w]hen the apparent size of the moon changes, along with it the apparent position of the observer changes" (Ihde 2004: 141). This is, of course, an illustration of what Ihde means by relativistic ontology vis-à-vis technologies. Technologies create new relations, and relations of relations, which, in turn, produce new worlds.

Rethinking worlds beyond phenomenology

The thinkers just discussed – Berger, Eliade, Heidegger, and Ihde – all share a common language of "worlds" due in large part to their intellectual debt to phenomenology. Husserl's original definition of "lifeworld" leaves the door open for the possibility of it being merely ideological (to recall Milbank's critique of Berger). This could result in a couple of problems. First, religion and/or technologies can be viewed as merely symbolically effective vis-à-vis the human being, producing an intellectualized understanding of both. Thus, the study of a religion as lifeworld can remain at the level of the symbolic pertinence of religion. Likewise, the study of technology as lifeworld would remain at the level of its effect on the consciousness of the human subject.

Additionally, religion and technologies, when viewed as "world-constructors," are seen as being so in a totalistic fashion. The worlds of religion and the worlds of technologies are complete, whole, and neat, mirroring the "closed system" of thermodynamics. Cosmology and ontology, for the most part, are conceived as closed systems. The human being or subject within this structured, ordered, and unified world would have very little interpretive recourse except the development of *Weltanschauung* or worldview that would correlate

42   *From cosmos to sphere*

with the *Weltbild*. In principle, there is nothing misguided or wrong about this approach. However, it does tend to slide into, what Jacques Derrida, in another context, called, "structurality" (Derrida 1991). One of the features of structurality is the tendency for ahistoricism and dogmatism. Worlds, whether they be Ihdian bodily-perceptual lifeworlds, Heideggerian "object spheres," Eliadian sacred cosmoses, or the Bergerian *nomoi* become worlds in and of themselves. This then excludes the possibility of "religion" or "technologies" – depending on which is given analytical privilege as world-constructor – interacting with other forces of social life. Religion and technology become identitarian, stable entities. But lest we forget, as Stewart Hoover reminds us, religion must not be seen as "given" but rather as achieved (Hoover 2006). This must therefore also extend to when we attempt to understand religion and technology, respectively, as "worlds." Such worlds must be achieved. Thus, in order to take into consideration technology and religion and their "worldhoods" seriously, what kind of "world" must we be talking about?

To approach this question, it will be useful to look at the work of two contemporary theorists of worlds – Jean-Luc Nancy and Peter Sloterdijk. Both authors offer a unique set of concepts that help us to place "world" and "cosmos" in a new historical light, thus allowing us to steer a different course from the theories of world-construction laid out in the authors discussed above.

Nancy traces the view of the world as ordered and structured from the Roman "*Urbi et orbi*" (from Rome to the world), a phrase that today embodies the very notion of "political theology." Once the opening statement for official decrees in ancient Rome, it is today used to refer to a papal address. As another Rome-related phrase, "All roads lead to Rome," would also indicate, this view of the world is centered on a *singular, privileged origin*. Though the dissolution of the Byzantine Empire in the fifteenth century had all but eliminated the Roman Empire in its political form, the remnants of the Imperium lived on in European colonialism. As Nancy points out, the figure of "the West" was the new Rome that functioned under the logic of *Urbi et orbi* until the decolonization movements of the 1950s–1970s initiated by India's liberation from the British in the late 1940s (Nancy 2007: 34). What decolonization challenged in particular were the twin values that undergirded this model of the world – the universal and reason, ideals promised to much of the colonized world in the gift wrap of progress and modernity, but not delivered to the extent pledged. When this was rejected, the world of *Urbi et orbi* was as well.

Sloterdijk goes further back than Nancy, pointing to the Greeks as respon-sible for introducing the idea of "sphere." The "sphere," which he interestingly uses interchangeably with "cosmos," is the earliest instance of the idea of globalization in the West, the contemporary "vectors" of which, he suggests, are "rapid transportation as well as ultra-high-speed telecommunication." Greek philosophical cosmology, by which Sloterdijk is quite clearly referring to the Aristotelian variety, theorized the cosmos as a response, so he claims,

From cosmos to sphere 43

to the fact that human beings could no longer live in a real cosmos, that is, a "closed and comforting world," which "was the totality of being imagined under the form of a great, perfectly symmetrical bubble" (Sloterdijk 2005: 223). As our discussion of Eliade already made clear, cosmization is the equation of house and universe in order to make a space inhabitable in Western and non-Western cultures. Sloterdijk describes this as "the great simplifying maneuver" in that it set in motion a view of "world" and thus "globalization" as rooted in ordering (as Berger's *nomos* does).

> If the house is the cosmos, and if the cosmos is the house of man, then the notion of habitat is extended to all the forces of chaos that subverted the ancient order of things. The pre-philosophical universe was much more threatened by chaotic forces than the well-arranged cosmos of the post-Platonists. After the age of Plato and Aristotle, the world became a cultivated garden surrounding the villa of an aristocrat jovially observing the totality of things from his terrace.
>
> (Sloterdijk 2005: 239)

The ancient cosmology of concentric circles, which had a major influence on Ptolemy, creates a "symbolic immune system" whereby the foundations of social knowledge are based on the whole and closed nature of the world. Sloterdijk and Nancy, both, move away from the concepts of ancient (Greco-Roman) cosmology to analyze the contemporary situation, which for purposes of this project, will have special attention paid to religion and new media technologies.

Therefore, "world" for Nancy signifies:

> a totality of meaning ... to which certain meaningful content or a certain value system properly belongs in order of knowledge or thought as well as in that of affectivity and participation. Belonging to such a totality consists in sharing this content and this totality in the sense of "being familiar with it," as one says; that is to say, of apprehending its codes and texts, precisely when their reference points, signs, codes, and texts are neither explicit nor exposed as such.
>
> (Nancy 2007: 42)

While at first glance it seems that Nancy is giving a phenomenological definition of the world, there is a particular aspect of "world" that he points out, which separates his definition from the others outlined above – "affectivity and participation." The aspect of "familiarity," as he calls it, stakes out an important difference between the Nancian "world," and the phenomenological "world" of Peter Berger. Whereas Berger's world may be reliant upon human consciousness, Nancy's, to the contrary, is rooted in a *bodily* familiarity much in the way of Ihde's "lifeworld." This familiarity does not necessarily reflect upon a symbolic system, which would lead to a portrait of "world" as given

44 *From cosmos to sphere*

and ready-made for consciousness to perceive, but something that is not exactly conscious. However, as we can see from Nancy's more detailed formulation of world and world-forming especially, it betrays a certain *non*-objectivity.

> [A] world is not a unity of the objective or external order: a world is never in front of me, or else it is my world. As soon as a world appears to me as world, I already share something of it: I share a part of its inner resonances. Perhaps this term *resonance* is capable of suggesting the issue at hand: a world is a space in which a certain tonality resonates. But that tonality is nothing other than the totality of resonances that the elements, the moments, and the places of this world echo, modulate, and modalize.
>
> (Nancy 2007: 42)

A world, therefore, is a world only for those who "inhabit" it, as he says. It is a place that allows events to take place. The non-objectivability of the world means that the world is not assigned a particular principle of telos. It rejects the "enframing" of the *Weltbild*.

The world, in this framework, also has theological consequences. A representable world is a world with God as "subject of its representation (and thus of its fabrication, of its maintenance and destination)" as the earlier discussion of the clockmaker analogy makes clear (Nancy 2007: 44). To represent the workings of nature was to reflect God. This correlation is traceable to the beginnings of Western metaphysics in the ancient Greek *Logos, ultima ratio* and *causa prima* which Thomas Aquinas most successfully translated into Christianity (see Maritain 2006). However, a world that cannot be represented is one that rejects not only this correlation but also a certain specific vision of God, that is, God as creator.

Furthermore, how this world is formed, "creation" in Nancian parlance, is a flat-out rejection of the given.

> The idea of creation, such as has been elaborated by the most diverse and at the same time most convergent thoughts, including the mystics of the three monotheisms but also the complex systems of all great metaphysics, is above all the idea of *ex nihilo* (and I do not exempt Marx from this, to the contrary: while his understanding of Christian creation is only instrumental, for him value is precisely created...). The world is created from nothing: this does not mean fabricated with nothing by a particularly ingenious producer, and not even coming out of nothing (like a miraculous apparition), but in a quite strict manner and more challenging for thought: the nothing itself, if one can speak in this way, or rather *nothing* growing [croissant] as *something* (I say "growing" for it is the sense of *cresco* – to be born, to grow – from which comes *creo:* to make something merge and cultivate a growth). In creation, a growth grows from nothing and this nothing takes care of itself, cultivates its growth.
>
> (Nancy 2007: 51)

From cosmos to sphere 45

I present Nancy's and Sloterdijk's post-Heideggerian theory of worlds to suggest that it offers a more suitable framework for this study in light of two realities. They both offer a stronger theory of world and world-forming (or, "creation" as Nancy calls it, and "spherology" as Sloterdijk calls it) and it gives us a more appropriate framework to analyze the relation of contemporary religion and media technologies. On the one hand, the notion of religion can no longer be simply thought of as ideological or symbolic, as the producer of meaning and context for the human mind. This kind of conception of world too easily falls into an immaterial theory of religion, akin to the overtly anti-religious approaches to the study of religion exhibited in Freud and Feuerbach before him. On the other hand, the study of technologies as world-forming thus far outlined do not take into full consideration the distinct break that digitization has initiated in the history of media technologies. The kinds of world occasioned by digital (or new), post-modern media technologies are indeed different than those Enframed by the modern technologies.

The type of world occasioned by digital, post-modern media technology can be described using Deleuze's term "plane of immanence" (Deleuze 1997). All prior media, in this sphere, become interoperable and virtually interactive with current media through digitization. Describing this as the "pseudo-religious" effect of digital media, Pierre Levy refers to this as "universalization," which he distinguishes from totalization. The universality of new media, for instance, the World Wide Web, "lacks any center or guidelines. It is empty without any particular content. Or rather, it accepts all content, since it can connect any point with any other, regardless of the semantic load of the entities so related" (Lévy 2001: 91). The disjuncture of the universal and totality occurs through a "world-forming" process, facilitated by digital technologies. Levy refers to this as the creation of a "shared context." As Levy writes, "We are all in the same bath, the same communicational deluge" (Lévy 2001: 100). The Web is a prime example of the ability to universalize without totalizing, a feature which has deep resonance with Nancy's *mondialization* and "creation." They both feature an openness and non-teleological quality that is present in a great deal of the literature of worlds in religious studies and the philosophy of technology.

It is a theory of "worlding" linking religion and technology, informed by the "universalizing yet non-totalizing" nature of digitization, which can be found in philosopher Mark Taylor's *After God*. What distinguishes Taylor's approach is that he shies away from a definition of religion. Instead, pointing to the "pressing conflicts resulting from uncertainties and instabilities created by globalization," Taylor states that there must be a renewed direction in religious studies that moves away from modern categories of classification and interpretation (Taylor 2007: 10). Not only do they fail to aid us in interrogating the ways in which they are cast for political ends but also fail to consider the changing nature of what we call "religion," not to mention its interrelation with other areas of life. What is necessary is a new way of thinking not only religion but also systems of all kinds – biological, social, political, cultural, and technological – and how they resonate in different ways. He writes:

46　*From cosmos to sphere*

> [N]etworks as well as their interrelations are, in different ways, information-processing systems, which, when fully deployed, are global: everything – absolutely everything – is entwined, enmeshed, interrelated, interconnected. Within these coevolving networks, different systems codetermine each other. Cultural systems, for example, condition natural systems as much as natural systems influence cultural systems. Religious attitudes shape values, which issue in political and economic policies that literally transform the fabric of life ... Far from a simple biological force, life is a complex global network of natural, social, economic, political and cultural relations. To sustain life it is necessary to cultivate all of these relations. As connections proliferate and relations multiply, the network of life becomes increasingly complex. This complexity produces instabilities that are the condition of the infinite restlessness of life itself.
>
> (Taylor 2007: 343)

Hence, for Taylor, the task of studying religion today must include these two facts: religion must be seen as enmeshed and implicated in "milieux" of other systems, as he calls it, and it must be considered as coevolving, that is, it is not a static entity or system but adaptive and dynamic. Thus, Taylor's "definition" of religion is reflective of these concerns.

> Religion is an emergent, complex, adaptive network of symbols, myths, and rituals that, on the one hand, figure schemata of feeling, thinking, and acting in ways that lend life meaning and purpose and, on the other, disrupt, dislocate, and disfigure every stabilizing structure.
>
> (Taylor 2007: 12)

To conceptualize religion-as-network is not to study a *set* or a *system* of beliefs, symbols, and rituals, at least not stable ones but rather a *network* of beliefs, symbols, and rituals that are most likely in flux. The phenomenon of "religion" can be thought as the way in which "theology, anthropology and cosmology mutually condition each other." It is for this reason that Taylor analyzes religion as a particular kind of symbolic network, one that has existential or ontological consequences. It is a network that not only puts into play various symbols and rituals but also the key ontological relations of the self, world, and God. He gives an example of this dynamic of what he calls the "religious network."

> [T]raditionally there have been two alternatives within the parameters of this vision: either God's will follows God's reason, in which case the world is ultimately comprehensible, or God's will is antecedent to reason, in which case the world is radically contingent and irreducibly mysterious ... When religion is understood as a complex adaptive network, it becomes clear that these contrasting theological alternatives are coimplicated in

From cosmos to sphere   47

such a way that neither can be itself apart from the other and each becomes itself in and through the other.

(Taylor 2007: 22)

Similarly, technology, Taylor argues, also reflects the emergent character of complex networks. Like religion, technology is not simply a set of objects or ideologies but it "grow[s] out of and act[s] back upon natural, social, and cultural systems."

> If natural, social, cultural processes are, in effect, distributed information processes, then the digital revolution is creating technologies whose structure and function not only reflect but more importantly amplify and transform what is already occurring in the world. When information machines are connected in webs that have the same structure as national, social and cultural systems, coevolution becomes inevitable even if its direction is impossible to predict.
>
> (Taylor 2007: 30)

We can see that Taylor's theory of religion and of technology is rooted in a concept of relationality. Religion and technology are each relational networks, and have the ability to produce new situations and contexts by putting into play different systems and networks. We can see an example of such relationality between the networks of religion and technology in the work of political theorist William Connolly on American evangelicalism and the right-wing media. In "The Evangelical-Capitalist Machine" (Connolly 2005), Connolly argues that the alliance forged between American-style capitalism, what he calls "cowboy capitalism," and evangelical Christianity cannot be "understood through the terms of efficient causality, in which you first separate factors and then show how one is the basic cause, or how they cause each other or how they together reflect a more basic cause" (Connolly 2005: 869). He suggests that their respective "spiritual dispositions" for "ruthlessness, ideological extremism, and readiness to defend a market ideology" are made explicit, or "actualized" by media.

> The complex becomes a powerful machine as evangelical and corporate sensibilities resonate together, drawing each into a larger movement that dampens the importance of doctrinal differences between them. At first, the parties sense preliminary affinities of sensibility; eventually they provoke each other to transduct those affinities into a massive political machine. And the machine then foments new intensities of solidarity between these constituencies.
>
> (Connolly 2005: 871)

Thus, instead of using Taylor's relational approach, Connolly uses the term "resonant" to describe the intertwining of American capitalism and evangelical Christianity. To be sure, this resonance defies any sort of causal model of

48   *From cosmos to sphere*

explanation. In this particular example, an unstable third entity exists: a *dispostif* made up of twenty-four-hour cable news television, the right-wing blogosphere and the vast circulation of funds. This third is unstable because it does not resemble the traditional "thirds" in the history of philosophy. For instance, in Hegelian dialectics, the third is a stable entity, one that is a product of two prior stable entities. The third, in the case of the evangelical-capitalist resonance machine, is neither singular nor bound; it is, on the contrary, a modular network of different media technologies, with "diverse elements [that] infiltrate into the others, metabolizing into a moving complex" (Connolly 2005: 870). It is an assemblage. Resonance stands in nearly direct opposition to causality, which as a model of understanding relationships, usually assumes stable and self-contained entities. Ontologically speaking, "self-containment" is, as far as Connolly is concerned, an outmoded and ultimately unhelpful way of approaching objects and their relationships. So how do we describe intermingling of any kind without causality?

Connolly suggests we use "affinities." Affinities are always virtual, that is, they are potential connections that in the proper conditions and settings could attach to one another. Connolly rightly describes them as "sensibilities" (Connolly 2005: 873). Doctrines, on the contrary, are codified systems of belief, which are more difficult to reconcile, as they necessitate almost strict adherence. To understand why he argues this, we must return to his emphasis on the figure of the machine in order to further examine his theory of media, which is at the heart of his notion of resonance. According to Connolly, media (by which he only means TV and film, oddly) that present "much of their work below the level of explicit attention and encourage the intense coding of those experiences as they do so," leave the viewer mostly "immobilized before a moving image and sound track, while the everyday perceiver is either mobile or one step removed from mobility" (Connolly 2005: 880). It is the ability of media technologies to "activate" the affective capacities of its viewers/users vis-à-vis perceptual experience that is at the core of "resonance."

The work of Connolly, I suggest, can be seen as a concrete example and analysis of what Taylor describes as a complex, relational network. In showing the basis of the coming-together of religion, media and politics in the United States during the Bush era, Connolly terms the connective tissue of the evangelical-capitalist resonance machine "affinities," or "sensibilities." Media, in this instance, news media, cannot be said to have simply done the work of causing or creating "cowboy capitalism." Rather, to the contrary, it effectively actualized certain features of religion and politics, decoding for the audience a particular affective, rather than semiotic, experience. Thus, networks, or spheres, are models of "worlding" rooted in sensibilities and affinities, rather than ideas, beliefs and doctrines.

Conclusion

Let us conclude with reminding ourselves again of the stakes. Why exert the effort to reconceptualize worlding, and with it ontology and cosmology in

From cosmos to sphere 49

relation to religion and technology? Quite simply, it is because the worlding of contemporary religiosity takes on a distinctly different flavor than the totalizing models of "cosmos" that mid-century sociology and history of religion largely purported. It is the theory of worlds, as "relational network" and "resonance machine," informed by digitization, which I believe to be operating in the theological conceptualization and practical use of digital technologies in contemporary American Protestantism, especially among multisite churches. It is in the digital networks of today's churches, including the technologized media environment of worship spaces and the extensive use of online social media – the subject of the following two chapters – where I believe we can see most clearly the distinctly digital convergence of religion and new media technologies.

3 (Atmo)sphere

The liturgical aesthetics of deterritorialized worship spaces

Introduction

My parents used to live in a suburb of New York City in the neighboring state of New Jersey. The church they used to attend, of which my father was an elder, is typical of the successful Korean congregations in the New York metropolitan area, sometimes called "the Tri-State." In 2005, after experiencing rapid growth in terms of attendance and membership (in turn, funds), the church, like many others of its kind, undertook a construction project to redesign its building, which was previously an office complex.

One Sunday, during a spring break (it must have been Easter), when I was back at their house, I noticed that the church was no longer an office building with a cross in front of it – which it had been – but something resembling a "megachurch." While the term is usually reserved for churches with congregations consisting of upwards of 2,000 weekly worshipers (which my parents' church was quite close to having) and usually associated with evangelicalism (their church is Presbyterian in affiliation), I use it not so much to refer to the sheer number of congregants or the theological leanings but the architectural and technological elements of the space.

Though it retained much of the office-building feel on the exterior, the interior is what made it seem, in my estimation, a megachurch. The worship hall or chapel was enormous, probably able to hold close to a thousand people at a time. But this was not all that noteworthy. The outside was big; of course the inside would be too. But being an observer of technology, I was most impressed by the lighting, audio, and video system that had been newly installed. Having worked as a chief sound engineer during college as part of my work-study, as well as someone who had spent much time in his youth in churches, technical rigs at many houses of worship and even professional music venues, for that matter, did not easily impress me. This one did. There were floating speakers, a theater-grade lighting setup, on-stage audio monitors, and *two* projection screens – one behind the altar, in view of the worshipping audience, and one on the back wall, allowing those on stage to see a different video feed than the congregants. (I found this to be particularly clever.)

At the start of the service, I heard the band play some contemporary Christian praise song that sounded mildly familiar. The band, to my surprise, *sounded* good. By this I am not referring to the skill or talent of the musicians but the *mix* sounded good. The vocalists and the instruments were equalized (EQ'd) properly, with each element clearly audible and in balance, not drowned out by one another. Previously, I had witnessed so many church bands play in my life with such poor setups that made them sound less than professional. To hear this one sound so good and so clear, and not muddled by the poor acoustics of a church, was indeed a great shock.

This shock is something that is not widely shared for many young Christians in the United States. For those who attend what are euphemistically called "contemporary" worship services, this level of technological sophistication and investment is not at all remarkable. Many churches, like that of my parents, now have two or more services with differing styles. Usually, the earlier service is more traditional, sticking closer to a traditional liturgy and using hymns. Older members of the church usually attend this service. The later service does not follow a traditional liturgy. There is emphasis on "praise," a time where a band, alternatively called praise team, leads the congregation in contemporary worship songs. These are not subject to the power structure of a denomination, as in the case of hymnals. The projection screen is crucial for this style of worship. The lyrics of the songs are projected onto the screen using computer software similar to Microsoft PowerPoint, like EasyWorship, which is specifically designed for this very purpose, as well as Mediashout and ProPresenter.

From mega to multi

The emergence of "megachurches" is difficult to track. Its very definition arouses some consternation among sociologists and others who keep an eye on religion. Are they purely defined by numbers? Is there a unified theology among all megachurches? What about worship? Is there a consistent worship style through all megachurches? These sorts of questions are doomed for failure, or so it seems. Yet, some of the most prominent megachurch watchers have attempted, with various degrees of success, to create a unified definition of megachurches. One prominent report on megachurches, by Scott Thumma and Warren Bird of the Hartford Institute for Religion Research, defines a megachurch as a Protestant church that draws at least 2,000 worshipers in a typical weekend (Thumma and Bird 2008). Although the report goes on to describe in greater detail some of the shared characteristics of these churches, there is, nevertheless, an *a priori* quantitative definition of the megachurch. This is rather unfortunate as the report contains some key insights into the changing nature of megachurches – especially when it comes to how they use technology and worship style.

The term "megachurch" emerged in mainstream American discourse around the late 1980s. A simple search in the archives of *The New York*

52 *(Atmo)sphere*

Times reveals that the term appears with great frequency right around 1989. There were of course large-attendance churches in the US prior to the 1980s. Robert Schuller's Crystal Cathedral, which seats over 2,500, comes to mind. While megachurches are no longer a novelty on the American religious landscape, what has emerged in the scholarship, specifically in the sociology of religion, is a consensus that megachurches, in addition to being a "type" of church, is also a *logic*, that is, a cluster of ideas about "doing church." It features most prominently a "contemporary worship style," which includes the use of particular technologies such as musical instruments (guitars, keyboards, and crucially a video projection screen), as in my parents' church.

But more recently, within the last eight years, according to Thumma and Bird's report, there has also been a rise in "the creation of...multiple sites to hold additional worship services under a single identity, unified budget and solo senior leader" (Thumma and Bird 2008: 6). These multisite churches have taken the mantle from megachurches and have, in my view, intensified the features of megachurches. The Barna Research Group, which produces studies primarily "pertaining to spiritual development, and facilitates the healthy spiritual growth of leaders, children, families and Christian ministries" (Barna Group 2008), stated in a recent report that two-thirds of Protestant churches currently have a large screen projection system that they use for services and other events. This is a huge jump from 2000, when just 39 percent of Protestant churches stated that they had such a system.

Many of the churches within that percentage, according to a National Public Radio report in 2005, were using technology to branch out and attempt to become "multi-site" (Ludden 2005). These churches use technology to maintain some form of continuity between the central church and the satellite churches. This is done through "simulcasting" aspects of worship services through large projection screens and heavy online ministry, including online church, podcasts, email, and social networking site presence among other things, which will be explored in the following chapter in greater detail.

Multisite churches have become a bit of a fault line in some Christian circles, not only because of the capitalist franchising model that it seems to mirror, but also because of its intense incorporation of technology in all aspects of ministry. Numerous articles and books have appeared in recent times taking stock of "the multisite movement" (Surratt 2009). Some of the criticisms, predictably, raise questions about pastoring: "How can a preacher pastor his flock when he cannot possibly know or meet every member of his church?" one article asks (Barnhart 2008). Many Christian leaders and pastors raise similar concerns about multisite as they do with megachurches – the potential for the development of a cult of celebrity preacher. The same article quotes a pastor who says, "When the video service decision is made, there is a conscious decision made by the leadership that the personality (or teaching) of one man is more important than meaningful connection with the audience."

For churches that are large and wealthy enough, the most immediate matter of course is, as the Barna report states, the installation of an audiovisual (A/V) system in the main worship space. Having a high-tech worship space is, for these churches, crucial to providing a contemporary worship experience. This is considered necessary for church growth, and is seen as one of the ways in which a church can attract newer (and younger) members. But, as leaders and thinkers associated with the church growth movement and those who have not established official relationships with it but certainly do consider growth an important part of their church's mission, it is usually couched in terms of creating a technologically infused worship space, and with it, an engaging (read: young, more contemporary) worship experience. For them, space transmits specific ideas about the "culture" of the church. As one professor of theology writes, "What values does your ministry facility communicate? Are they values you intend to communicate? What's your theology of space?" (Metzger 2009).

The analytic of space

The study of religious communities has in the tradition of Durkheimian anthropology and sociology entailed, as a French sociologist of religion writes, "the study of the relations that each religious community maintains with the space in which it has become established" (Hervieu-Léger 2002: 99). In other words, to study religion is also to analyze the relationship to the world that has been formalized theologically. Hence, religious community and spatiality are, in some ways, co-constituted. But in addition to this, as Hervieu-Leger rightly points out, there is another aspect to religious spatiality: the *symbolization* of space. "How does the religious imagination, with its dual components of memory and utopia, understand places?" she writes (Hervieu-Léger 2002: 100). Put differently, "religious spatiality" entails not only the relationship of the religious community to the world but also the very idea of place in the context of the belief system that "organizes the relations of a given religious community to its past and to its future" (Hervieu-Léger 2002: 100). One only needs to think of the City of God, Jerusalem, and Mecca, for examples.

The question of religious spatiality is further complicated by what Hervieu-Leger calls "religious modernity," referring to the contemporary state of religion, with the individualization of belief, the dismantling of mechanical solidarity bonds and the explosion of communication technologies. Today, there are "novel forms of religious sociability" (Hervieu-Léger 2002: 103). In particular, the "delocalization of the social and religious bond," which shuns collective forms of belief and institutional religion in favor of interpersonal relationships, has left a lasting mark on the modalities of religious communalization and spatiality. They now mirror what Troelstch once dubbed "spiritualismus" or "mystical networks," and are "continually reshaped" (Hervieu-Léger 2002: 103). These networks are the "chief modalities of a deterritorialized spatialization of the religious" (Hervieu-Léger 2002: 103). She summarizes the situation as such:

> A "bottom-up and top-down" type of spatialization, brought into play both by local mass gatherings and the spread of individual believers and by

54 *(Atmo)sphere*

> mobilization of the most modern communication technologies (even extending as far as the creation of virtual communities, completely detached from any form of local integration) and networking between dense cores of community, which is weaving new patterns of religion in space.
>
> (Hervieu-Léger 2002: 104)

Rather interestingly, Hervieu-Leger offers up the example of megachurches in the United States, which, in her estimation, illustrates "the dialectic of large gatherings that are not part of any overall plan and of the way proximity is being framed." This is, for her, typical of the "emergent forms of spatialization of the religious" in "advanced modernity" (Hervieu-Léger 2002: 104). I take seriously Hervieu-Leger's claim but also seek to extend her empirical aside to speak to issues more pertinent to this book, especially that of worlding and technology. Specifically, I suggest that Hervieu-Leger's linking of spatiality and communality in her argument regarding the "deterritorialized spatialization of the religious" is more readily demonstrated by current developments in American Christianity – namely multisite churches.

Therefore, in this chapter, I aim to suggest that a significant site of the deterritorialization of religious space that Hervieu-Leger mentions can be found in the technologized worship spaces of contemporary Christianity. An aspect of its deterritorialization is the reconstitution of spatiality – from something resembling a sacred enclosure to what Alex Wilkie has recently called a "people-technology configuration." I suggest that this reconstitution occurs through a dynamic and complex process whereby church architecture, digital technologies, and pastoral administrators come together and form a "regime of design" that constructs, following the work of Gernot Böhme, *atmosphere*. Religious space, therefore, is not the effect of a singularly identifiable cause nor is it the solution to a long equation of individually distinct forces. It is "heterogeneously composed [of] unities of interoperable elements" (Wilkie 2010: 10); it emerges out of "design practice, not pre-conditions." I ground this thesis in an examination of Bright Church, whose use of technology has been widely commented upon within and outside of Christian circles. I provide an experiential analysis of worship (and the digital technologies that facilitate it) at one of its dozen campuses, focusing on how the technologies impart a sense of connection and bonding with the pastor and other worshipers who are in distant locations through the formation of a "sphere." I argue that the resulting digital environment of the technologized worship space points towards a larger shift in ideas around Christian worship, which emphasizes embodiment and affectivity that are specifically actualized by digital, especially visual, environments.

A social theory of design

In order to elaborate this argument, I will draw from Bruno Latour's reading of Peter Sloterdijk's "spherology," which I'm calling a "social theory of design." For those who are familiar with Latour, it comes as no surprise that the

(Atmo)sphere 55

Sloterdijk-inspired theory of design put forth begins with the supposition that "the typically modernist divide between materiality on the one hand and design on the other is slowly being dissolved away" (Latour 2008: 2). By this, Latour intends to point out the extension of the concept of "design." Indeed, everything is now under design. At some of the most recognized art schools around the world, there are several tracks for studying design – industrial, product, interior, etc. This includes the designing of furniture to Nike sneakers. Thus, "design" has been delinked from its point of reference to apply to "cities, landscapes, nations, cultures, bodies, and genes ... and nature" (Latour 2008: 2).

Design, both philologically but also in contemporary use, means something like what it does in the original French – "relooking." It is to add a layer of form to a given creation, "a superficial feature that could make a difference in taste and fashion." To design is, therefore, to "redesign." It does not, according to Latour, "[begin] from scratch" (Latour 2008: 5). This, in turn, indicates a "deep shift in our emotional makeup" from originary or foundational thinking to something less totalistic. As he writes:

> at the very moment when the scale of what has to be remade has become infinitely larger ... what it means to "make" something is also being deeply modified ... things are no longer "made" or "fabricated," but rather carefully designed.
>
> (Latour 2008: 4)

It is this aspect of the term "design," which Deleuze and Guattari would undoubtedly call "repetition with a difference," that Latour finds to be the "antidote" to hubristic, modernist notions of "founding, colonizing, establishing" (Latour 2008: 5). What describes space as people-technology configuration most accurately is another set of modifiers: "enveloped, entangled, surrounded" (Latour 2008: 8). Deterritorialized space is not "a huge architecture" (Latour 2008: 9). This would betray a linear, top-down, causal understanding of the constitution of space. Instead, by understanding space as "designed," Latour is calling for a way of looking at space as "drawing things together – gods, nonhumans and mortals included" (Latour 2008: 13).

"Drawing together" is an apt description of Sloterdijk's sphere theory, although it may not so much be an accurate one. Much like Deleuze's Foucaultianism, Latour's Sloterdijkianism contains many aspects of the Frenchman's own vocabulary, in this case, of actor–network theory (Deleuze 1988). Famously for Latour's ontology, the idea of a stable object is non-existent. Objects contain a "network of concerns," or alternatively "a vast empire on information" (Latour 2011: 5). "Whenever you wish to define an entity," he says, "you have to deploy its attributes, that is, its network" (Latour 2011: 5). More impressionistically, he writes:

> Take any object: at first, it looks contained within itself with well delineated edges and limits; then something happens, a strike, an accident, a

56 *(Atmo)sphere*

catastrophe, and suddenly you discover swarms of entities that seem to have been there all along but were not visible before and that appear in retrospect necessary for sustenance.

(Latour 2011: 2)

Thus, "drawing together" seems closer to "network" than "sphere."

Yet, along with Latour, I suggest that the "drawing together" reflects Sloterdijk's basic definition of the sphere – "structures of constitutive being-in-each-other and being-with-each-other" (Sloterdijk 2011: 544). Both sphere and network are predicated on the rejection of edges and limits, in other words, enclosed and discreet totalities. As discussed in the previous chapter, Sloterdijk wages the brunt of his critique of "the Western metaphysics of roundness" on a singular figure – the globe. The globe, that perfectly round and enclosed shape, was introduced through Greek cosmology as a means by which to measure the immeasurable, and thus to place human beings within a totality. For him, it is this "originary philosophy" that gave rise to "mono-spherical thought." More significantly, it is "with this formalizing gesture, thinking individuals were bound to a strong relationship with the center of their existence and sworn to the unity, totality, and roundness of existence" (Sloterdijk 2009a: 31). The metaphysics of roundness, therefore, represents a fundamental misconception in Western thought where the "the unevenness of life and the fissures of the world must be measured" within "an encompassing zone," which is no longer a house but a "logical and cosmological construction form of timeless validity" (Sloterdijk 2009a: 31).

While the identification and critique of the metaphysics of roundness focus on the latter part of the phrase – the "together" of "drawing together" – the "drawing" part is also of importance in Latour's use of Sloterdijk, primarily as it pertains to what one refers to as "digitality" (Latour 2011: 8) and the other as "virtual space of cybernetic media" (Sloterdijk 2011: 66). To draw has two meanings, especially as it pertains to "design." On the one hand, it refers to the rather obvious attempt at making a picture through marks. On the other hand, there is "to draw in," to pull, to attract. Both meanings are operative here. Digitization provides a socio-technological analogue that describes the social ontology for which Latour and Sloterdijk, both of whom I'm suggesting are contributing to the "social theory of design," are attempting to clear a path. In particular, both "network" and "sphere" upend traditional dicho-tomies of whole/part as well as its cognates such as universal/particular and society/individual. But this is played out differently in Sloterdijk than in Latour. Sloterdijk identifies the chief characteristic of this new virtuality as a generalized decentering. "When everything has become the center," Sloterdijk writes, "there is no longer any valid center; when everything is transmitting, the allegedly central transmitter is lost in the tangle of messages" (Sloterdijk 2011: 71). Latour, in a decidedly un-Derridean move, argues that "every individual is part of a matrix whose lines and columns are made of others as well" (Latour 2011: 13). Models that adhere to two (hierarchical) levels, such

(Atmo)sphere 57

as the Platonic one, preclude the possibility of the parts being bigger than the whole. Hence, society is always viewed as "superior" to individuals in mainstream social science.

The name that Latour gives this social ontology is of course "the network." But unlike the understanding of networks popularized by Manuel Castells of "multiple nodes," which emphasizes connectivity, Latour, in language close to that of Taylor covered earlier in the previous chapter, plays up the empty spots in the image of the net. It represents, he writes, "the subversion" of "universality."

> The area "covered" by any network is "universal" but just as long and just where there are enough antennas, relays, repeaters, and so on, to sustain the activation of any work.
>
> (Latour 2011: 8)

Networks are, he continues, composed "mainly of voids...[Its] universality is fully local" (Latour 2011: 8).

The name that Sloterdijk gives this form of life is "foam" or "bubble." The foam bubble is "an architectural foam, a multi-chambered system made up of relatively stabilized personal worlds" (Sloterdijk 2009b). The metaphor of foam reflects the fact that worlds have always had plural and insular structures. Elsewhere, he describes foam as guided by the "morphological principle of the polyspheric world", as not being a *singular* world but *multiple* worlds. In doing so, he evokes the language of "networks" and "media."

> The structural implication of the current earth-encompassing network – with all its eversions into the virtual realm – is thus not so much a globalization as a foaming. In foam worlds, the individual bubbles are not absorbed into a single, integrative hyper-orb, as in the metaphysical conception of the world, but rather *drawn together* to form irregular hills.
>
> (Sloterdijk 2011: 71, emphasis added.)

In this sense, foam theory is a polycosmology (Sloterdijk 2009b: 8).

I will show below that worship spaces in multi-site churches can be thought of as relational networks, foams or spheres, in which people and technology are drawn together–in the sense of both picturing and attracting–in a regime of design resulting in an aesthetics of worship (or "liturgical aesthetics") that emphasizes sensory, affective experience. It does so, I demonstrate, through a strategy of universalization without totalization.

Bright Church

Started in 1996, Bright Church, according to some sources, is one of the largest Protestant churches in America, with most current numbers placing it as having somewhere between 38,000 and 40,000 members across thirteen

58 (Atmo)sphere

campuses in the US (Grossman 2009). It exemplifies the ethos of multisite par excellence. Denominationally, it is affiliated with the very small evangelical denomination, according to Conrad Gottschalk, founder and senior pastor of Bright Church.[1] While many megachurches are indeed evangelical, multisite churches, as mentioned above, are characterized less than by their evangelicalism for their "style" or culture. Multisite churches tend to be younger, with many of the congregants ranging from ages 30 to 40. They also tend to be overwhelmingly white and middle class.

Besides its remarkable growth in numbers, Bright Church has garnered much press attention in the past decade due to its heavy use of new media technologies in both its physical worship spaces as well as the launch of its Online Campus, which meets strictly online. While many churches use technologies in order to serve their growth model, Bright Church has, in many ways, built its entire raison d'être around technology. This is largely attributable to its multisite character.

Being multisite poses similar technological challenges for all churches, not just Bright Church. They tend to revolve around liturgy. How will the message (sermon) be transmitted – satellite? pre-recorded video files? How much of the worship will rely on satellite feed and how much will be in-person? How will the music be played? In addition to these liturgical challenges, there are other challenges, related to what Christians call "fellowship." How does a church with several different campuses create a feeling of one Church? How does it create a sense of "community"? As Christian theologians remind us, these two sets of questions are not in any way mutually exclusive. Not only do many liturgies include the reinforcement of "community," for instance, in the communal reading of The Apostles' Creed, a staple of many Western Christian traditions, but they are by their very being, a means of connecting the individual church to the universal church. Thus, the study of technology in worship spaces necessarily includes the dual focus on liturgy and ecclesiology.

Let us look at how this unfolds in a particular religious setting, Bright Church's upstate New York campus. The New York campus, in addition to being one of Bright Church's newer campuses, is also among its smallest. Of the roughly 26,000 who attend one of the thirteen campuses of Bright Church every week, the New York campus only makes up 2 percent (MacAngus 2010). Its pastoral staff consists of just two pastors – the campus pastor and worship pastor. The campus pastor's duties are what we would traditionally associate with the senior pastor of a given congregation. The worship pastor is responsible for all of the technical ins and outs of the church. At Bright Church–New York, this turns out to be quite a bit, as much of the worship service, which Bright Church across the board calls "experience," is wholly reliant upon the smooth functioning of various technologies.

Bright Church–New York's worship space, while small, seating only 200 congregants at a time, is nevertheless a digital media environment–a sphere. One of the first things that worshipers, who come to one of the two

(Atmo)sphere   59

experiences on a given Sunday, see to their right is the large tech booth, where the audio/visual/lighting equipment are all stored.

Towards the front, where the stage, not sanctuary, is, are three screens – one dropdown projection screen and two large television monitors flanking it on either side. When you look up, there are flying speakers (in audio technology parlance, this means hanging from the ceiling) and spotlights as well as numerous acoustic panels hanging down to counteract some of the sonic inconsistencies of the dome-shaped ceiling. On the side of the stage are two "intelligent," or moving, lights that, like their name suggests, are able to swivel and move. A lighting board or software that is behind the tech booth controls their movement.

On the stage itself are microphones, instruments, and amplifiers for the band, which consists of two guitars (one for rhythm, one for lead), a drum set behind an isolation screen, and a bass. Before the experience actually begins, background music plays over the speakers. Surprisingly, it is not Christian music. As the worship pastor Doug MacAngus explained to me, the pre- and post-worship music is always "secular music" as he put it. This, he says, is unique to Bright Church. "Because we have the person who isn't familiar with church in mind," he tells me (MacAngus 2010). At 9:30 or 11:00, the two experience start times, MacAngus and his band take the stage. He then asks everyone to stand. Usually, their first song is a secular song, a "cover" – sometimes a top 40 hit, sometimes a song like the theme to the Ghostbusters movie.

After this, a video plays on all three screens simultaneously, announcing, "The Bright Church Experience begins now," flashy with animated graphics hitting from all angles. Center, left, and right, even one's peripheral vision cannot wrest free of the grip of the graphics. It is at this exact moment that the media environment truly turns on. It is a cosmogonic moment; it is the creation of the techno-religious sphere. All of the technical elements are set into motion. The house lights are dimmed, and the lighting system goes into full effect.

It is no wonder that Bright Church adamantly calls their worship services "experiences." As Jeremy Sitz, Bright Church's Head of Innovation, relayed to me, "It is intentional. It's not service. We're trying to help you experience God" (Sitz 2010).

During the eighteen minutes or so that the praise time happens, MacAngus' wife, who controls all of the video aspects, uses software called ProPresenter in order to project the lyrics of the praise songs as well as background images that resemble stock desktop wallpaper images on computers. ProPresenter, made by a company called Renewed Vision, is a "professional worship presentation" tool. It allows "an operator to control a presentation on one screen, while dynamically affecting the visuals and lyrics experienced by an audience on one or more screens," as it states on its website. The operator at Bright Church–New York uses ProPresenter to time the display of the lyrics much in the way that karaoke lyrics are displayed but in this case manually (though ProPresenter does have an automation function). The background images

60 *(Atmo)sphere*

seem to be pre-selected based on the lyrics and "feel" (i.e. tempo) of the song. For up-tempo, energetic songs, the images behind the lyrics tend to move at a faster pace and during slower songs, they tend to be more static.

During all of this, another staff member (not volunteers as all of the tech and band members are paid) is controlling the lighting system using a design system called Vista, made by a company called Jands. There are several packages on the market, some which include both hardware (a physical console), but Bright Church–New York uses the software-only package. The lighting designer sits behind a computer to control the lights through a user interface that has all of the lighting components visually represented on a graphical replica of the space on the screen. From there, the user is able to adjust the spreads, cross lights and cross fades throughout the experience. For example, while the praise team at the New York campus plays a particular song that includes the phrase, "In the darkness, God's light shines through," two intelligent lights on either side of the stage shoot beams of light directly towards the ceiling.

Meanwhile, the audio engineer, who MacAngus informs me, has gone on tour with many professional acts, sits behind the audio mixing board and computer. He is controlling the levels of the various instruments and vocalists but also supervising the backing track that is running through ProTools, which is a digital audio workstation that is used for both recording and performance settings. It is the industry standard and used in all Bright Church campuses. At Bright Church–New York, they run audio and video clips through ProTools. Prior to each weekend, MacAngus will have already selected which songs the band will "perform" (in many Christian circles, the worship band is seen not as performing but as "leading" worship). Because his band is, in his estimation, "bare bones," meaning there are not as many musical elements as he would like, he records many musical parts and plays alongside them in his "live" performances on Sundays. It makes the band "sound fuller," MacAngus says. This is facilitated by the use of in-ear monitors, with which the band members can all hear each other but also all of the instruments that are on the backing track, which is coming through ProTools. Of top priority, in any live musical performance with a backing track, is what is called "the click." The "click" is shorthand for click-track, which is a metronome that can be heard by all the performers with in-ear monitors but not the worshipping audience. This is important so that the recorded parts and played parts are all properly synced. If not, there would be a very noticeable clash.

At Bright Church, there is yet another reason for the click's importance – to make sure that the band keeps their worship set to exactly eighteen minutes. The experiences at Bright Church–New York, and indeed in all of Bright Church's campuses, are simultaneous, which is quite a feat since there are thirteen campuses as well as Church Online. This simultaneity is produced through a master clock, which is synced up to the Global Operations Center of Bright Church in the Plains. There, the master clock is set and synced up to all of the other clocks at the many campuses around the country. In order to ensure

(Atmo)sphere 61

that the "teaching" (sermon), which comes in live through satellite, starts at the right time, there are specific time markers to which the worship staff has to adhere. The first is at the 18-minute mark, at which the praise portion must stop. At this point, a spotlight hits the campus pastor Edward Coburn, who addresses the audience with a few welcoming words and asks the people who are there for the first time to fill out a "communication card." He must stop at the 21-minute mark because that is when the tech staff goes to the live satellite feed from the Global Operations Center.

Then, the spotlight fades away and a short film begins to play on all three screens. The picture quality is crisp; it is in HD (high definition). It is no longer than five minutes, and doubles as a transition into the message or "teaching" delivered by Craig Gottschalk, senior pastor of Bright Church, and an introduction. For this particular sermon, about how to deal with negative thoughts, the film depicts a group of people (some old, some young, some white, some black) walking into a white-walled room with permanent markers, who then proceed to write what are supposed to be disparaging things about themselves, such as "You are not skinny enough." After doing so, they walk out of the room.

After the short clip, which runs about five minutes, the teaching begins. The mise-en-scène consists of Gottschalk, equipped with a headset microphone, seated on a high stool, dressed in jeans and a polo shirt, with his sermon notes and Bible on a table beside him on the very large stage of the central Campus of Bright Church in the Plains. Behind him is a staged set, consisting of yellow container bins that say "toxic" on them, going along with the theme of the sermon series. While he delivers his sermon, or "teaching," camera angles are constantly changing. There is a moving camera along the base of the stage pointed upwards at him and there is a wide view as well as a single, probably mounted camera which he occasionally looks at directly, when he reaches a particularly important or emotional part of his sermon. This is facilitated through a technology called IMAG (image magnification), mentioned earlier.

Gottschalk is clearly a seasoned veteran when it comes to preaching not only to his immediate audience, but also to the cameras, without looking like he is cognizant of them. He is able to toggle this fine line of being media-trained and also seeming like a real person by using a variety of techniques to interact with the audience. For instance, he frequently takes straw polls, asking people in the attendance to raise their hands if, to use an example from the same sermon about negative thoughts, "they've ever felt debilitating doubt before." Quite surprisingly, the audience in the New York campus raised their hands even though a pastor fed in through a satellite feed was posing this question. A similar dynamic is at play when Gottschalk makes jokes, many of which are self-deprecating. In fact, like good preachers, his examples are autobiographical. He also makes it a point to make light of the fact that he is on-screen. At one point during a bit of a divergence in his sermon, he says that many people, when they meet him for the first time, say, "You're a lot smaller than I thought you'd be." He noted, "Just for the record. It's never good to hear that…in any

62 (Atmo)sphere

context," unafraid of sexual innuendo. This joke was especially a hit at the New York campus. Thus, there is a sense of comfort in the worship space as he preaches. I even saw couples with arms around each other and other worshipers furiously thumbing their mobile phones, tweeting or updating their Facebook status about the message.

During the teaching, the worshipers are seated and rapt in attention. It is quite hard to get bored while Gottschalk preaches. This speaks not really to the level of theological sophistication of his teaching but rather to the size and layout of the screens, as well as what they display. Throughout the teaching, visual aids appear whenever Gottschalk makes any reference to the Bible. The Bible verse to which he alludes appears below on a graphic strip, almost mimicking the running headlines on the bottom of the screen when one turns to CNN. Like a 24-hours cable news channel, there is a snazzy graphic that appears, which, in the case of this particular sermon, which was the first of a series called "Toxic," was a yellow biohazard triangle. It is assumed that worshipers do not need a Bible during worship. Gottschalk always says, "if you have your Bible, turn to…" For the worshipers of the New York campus, Gottschalk is clearly a familiar presence. The largeness and multiplicity of the images, projected on the central screen and the two television monitors, envelops the worshiper.

This, however, does not last throughout the duration of the experience. After the sermon, there is a transition into what is called, in evangelical churches, a "time of decision," alternatively known as "an altar call." During this time, soft, red lights hit the stage and soothing, droning electronic ambient music plays. (I peered over the audio engineer and the name of the song file was, in fact, "invitation music.") From behind the projection screen emerges Hodgins, the campus pastor, who speaks to the worshipers, asking if anyone is "wanting someone to pray" for them, clearly a "euphemization," as political anthropologist James Scott would put it (Scott 1989), to publicly display one's commitment to God and Jesus Christ "as his or her personal savior." This is the only "confrontational" part of the experience. If no one "comes to God," the campus pastor does a general prayer and goes onto a time of "giving," and ushers pass around several collection plates. These portions of the experience are presided upon by the New York campus pastor Eric Hodgins. Then the house lights dim and, across all three screens, another clip shows, showing the same white room with scrawled negative thoughts all across the walls. A man in a yellow HAZMAT suit walks in with a paint roller and tub of white paint. He proceeds to paint over the negative thoughts from earlier in the experience and walks out. The group that had originally written those things on the wall proceeds to write self-affirming statements on the walls. The house lights come up in the worship space and the experience ends.

Though I've only described a single worship experience at New York, there is good reason to believe that it is typical of all Bright Church's worship experience in all of its campuses. This is because not only are the teachings standardized but also nearly all of the technological aspects that facilitate the

(Atmo)sphere 63

worship experience are. This allows for easy troubleshooting, which is called for plenty of occasions, especially since Bright Church relies so heavily on technology. When there is an issue with the satellite feed or a syncing issue with audio, MacAngus, the worship pastor, calls a helpline and is guided through the problem remotely. This can only happen because the worship tech staff in Bright Church headquarters in Oklahoma is familiar with all of the equipment.

The continuity of experiences across the campuses is also ensured by its Global Operations Center (GOC). According to the project manager at Bright Church at the GOC:

> At the GOC, our leaders gather and watch the experiences at many of our campuses. This is accomplished by using a device at each campus call [sic] a Slingbox. We connect a camera, like a Sony HandyCam to the Slingbox and then connect the Slingbox to our network. With this setup, we are able to watch what is going live at our campuses in New York, Tennessee, Texas, Oklahoma, and Arizona.
>
> (Thomas 2008b)

Today, in the updated GOC, Bright Church leaders can watch up to ten experiences at the same time, while previously (at the time of the statement above), it could only support the watching of four or five. In addition, at the GOC, one is able to monitor the Online Campus (now called Church Online) but also the Attendance Management System, which shows "real-time attendance data from all the campuses" (Thomas 2008a). The GOC looks like the White House Situation Room, containing four television monitors, two on either side of a large projection screen, reminiscent of the layout of screens in the worship space of the campuses. The projection screen contains a 4×3 grid, with each box displaying the worship space of each campus. At the very bottom is the official clock that all of the campuses must organize their live components around. In fact, on the wall behind the tech booth in the New York campus is a digital clock with red letters, which is synced up to this clock. The central clock in software and other technologies that require syncing is called, appropriately enough, a "global clock."

The GOC is used, according to the project manager, to provide feedback and support after each experience. To be sure, however, there is undoubtedly, a tinge of surveillance as well. MacAngus states that the camera placed in the back of the worship space, which feeds a live stream to the Global Operations Center, is "lovingly" called "the Big Brother camera" by the worship staff at Bright Church–New York (MacAngus 2010). And to be sure, while this is fodder that feeds a Foucaultian nightmare, it is, at least for the particular interests of this chapter, evidence of the digital and imagistic method of Bright Church's sphere-forming.

Christian technological discourse

The alignment of church "culture," space, technology, and experience is clearly evident in Christian-oriented technology trade magazines and blogs.

64   *(Atmo)sphere*

Worship Facilities Magazine (*WFM*) and its parent magazine *Church Production Magazine* are by far the most prominent and most influential of these. Taken as an "order of discourse," we can see that in these publications there are certain trends and predominant ideas, the chief among them being that technologies, acting "architecturally," have the ability to create environments that affect a certain kind of religious experience. In nearly all of the articles and editorials that appear in *WFM* that deal with how church leaders can effectively create the ideal worship environment, the emphasis is quite often on experience. One editorial reads:

> Houses of worship are finding that A/V installations offer a dynamic and often cost-effective means of expanding reach and growing membership. Whether the systems installed are intended to *enhance the experience* within a single worship area or designed to deliver the worship message to a broader group at multiple sites, to web users, or to television audiences, the planning and execution of each of these projects is key to its immediate and long-term success.
>
> (Thompson 2009, emphasis added)

It continues to describe the thought-process behind a church considering investing in a new A/V system. After making sure to list the usual questions about the goals of the church meeting the budget of the project, it adds:

> Because worship is a very personal experience, the key considerations in planning an A/V installation within a house of worship extend beyond the technical. Though well-established congregations holding services in historic buildings may be most inclined to be protective of their facilities when looking at new A/V installs, all varieties of houses of worship must focus on maintaining the preeminence of the message while minimizing the presence of the technology that delivers the message.
>
> (Thompson 2009, emphasis added)

The back and forth, demonstrated here, between encouraging church leaders to invest in digital technologies but to also "ensure the message," is par for the course. The relationship between the perceived message and digital technologies is even considered by clearly pro-technology Christian writers as a negotiation. However, judging by the numerous articles and editorials found in these Christian-oriented technology blogs and magazines, there is, as in the italicized portion in the quotation above, a directive to blur the presence of technology into the background, that is, to the *environment* itself. Hence, the call to recede technology into the background is not only a way of negotiating sacred space but is also a latent theory of technology. Therefore, the above editorial is wrong when it states that planning for audio-visual equipment extends "beyond the technical." As I will show, technology decisions are made based on the interimplicated entanglement of architecture, space, technology, and, most importantly, worship experience.

In this particularly Christian technological discourse, a recurring theme regarding worship experience seems to center around the concept of transcendence. Worship spaces are ideally supposed to "create a space and a base to transform lives – sometimes quite subtly – and harness youthful energy, pointing it in a positive, even transcendent, direction" (Webb 2009). The most immediate means by which churches attempt to create a space conducive to a "transcendent experience" is through the use of video projection systems. Throughout the trade magazine literature, there is a detectable insistence on the mood-setting ability of projected images on large screens. No matter the image, it is the sheer size of the image that contributes most in the setting of the mood. Screens cannot only reach sizes usually associated with sports-arena JumboTrons, but the recent trend in large churches has been multiple screens. The screen's presence is perhaps the most imposing when one enters one of these environments.

In addition to the selection of images there is IMAG (image magnification), a technique used to provide live shots of the congregation on the projection screen throughout worship using cameras positioned in various places around the worship space. IMAG has roots in the entertainment industry, usually for events such as concerts, so that people seated far away can see what is happening on stage.

> The application of IMAG became popular in megachurches with the intent to *provide a sense of intimacy to the service (bringing the pastor closer to the congregation)*, where having the pastor "connect" with the congregation is very important. Initially, IMAG was rarely used in churches smaller than 1,500 seats or so. However, the technique has become more popular and its use is more widespread and effective in churches where there might be obstructed view seating (regardless of size). One might also see IMAG techniques applied in video venues or satellite churches where there is a local praise and worship band and other pastoral staff, while the senior or teaching pastor appears at the multiple locations via video.
>
> (Johnson 2010, emphasis added)

As the above notes, IMAG is used not simply for practical reasons (i.e. in order to allow the members in the space to see what is happening at the altar) but also for its ability to facilitate mood – in this instance, intimacy. IMAG does not isolate the individual worshiper-spectator but rather nudges him or her towards an affective experience of, what Max Scheler called, "fellow-feeling" (Scheler 2011). This is especially apparent when images of other worshipers appear on the screens. It provides a feeling of association, of "being-with" (*Mit-sein*). IMAG then is not so much a means of experiencing *individual* "transcendence," though it is largely described in such a way in this

66 *(Atmo)sphere*

order of Christian technological discourse, but the opposite; it induces a feeling of closeness and involvement, what Gernot Böhme would place under the heading of "atmosphere."

(Atmo)spheres: sensoria and spatiality

Atmosphere, as the philosopher Böhme states, is often indicative of "something indeterminate, difficult to express" (Böhme 1993: 113). It is difficult to figure out what to attribute atmosphere to – objects, environments or the very subjects who experience it? Moreover, while it is hard to pin down what atmosphere is, it seems, at least, for some reason, much easier to describe its "character", be it "serene, melancholic, oppressive, uplifting, commanding, inviting, erotic, etc." (Böhme 1993: 114). Yet, atmosphere is something we associate with certain spaces or environments but under specific contexts. For instance, Madison Square Garden in New York City is known as the "Mecca of Basketball." However, it would be difficult for any basketball fan to speak of Madison Square Garden in this way during a Bruce Springsteen concert being held there, for instance. "Mecca-ness" is not a constant feature of the Garden but only during times when basketball is the business being conducted there. Things are different when the Knicks play from when the Boss plays.

Böhme argues that this difference between these two scenarios can be thought of in direct relation to the aesthetics of environment and "things." By "things", Böhme means objects within the spatial environment. Things play a crucial part in the formation of atmosphere. They are not passive. They emit what he calls "ecstasies." To speak of ecstasy, Böhme is clearly referencing its philosophical usage, which usually connotes "being outside of oneself." This is often the description used by Christian mystics to describe their own experiences in trances and similar states. But objects, or "things" are ecstatic precisely because they "[take] away the homogeneity of the surrounding space and [fill] it with tensions and suggestions of movement" (Böhme 1993: 121). He explains, giving the example of a blue cup:

> The blueness of the cup is then thought of not as something which is restricted in some way to the cup and adheres to it, but on the contrary as something which radiates out to the environment … The existence of the cup is already contained in this conception of the quality "blue," since the blueness is a way of the cup being there, an articulation of its presence, the way or manner of its presence.
>
> (Böhme 1993: 121)

The blueness of the cup is at once a feature of the cup itself (that is to say, an internal dimension) as well as a feature of it in relation to its environment (that is to say, an external dimension). Although we cannot speak for the cup's specific effect on individual perceptions and moods, we can conclude that it contributes to the atmosphere by its very blueness. There is widespread

(Atmo)sphere   67

belief that rooms with blue walls are calming while those with red walls induce stress. While the research is hardly reliable or vast (Kutchma 2014; Kumarasamy *et al.* 2014), the perception of color is, in the world of interior design, closely associated with a certain kind of "affective impact" of a room's atmosphere. It is responsible for a kind of first perceptual impression. As Böhme writes, "the primary 'object' of perception is atmospheres" not "shapes or objects or their constellations" (Böhme 1993: 125). Or, as Giuliana Bruno states:

> Affects not only are markers of space but are themselves configured as space, and they have the actual texture of atmosphere. To sense a mood is to be sensitive to a subtle atmospheric shift that touches persons across air space. In this way, motion creates emotion and, reciprocally, emotion contains a movement that becomes communicated.
>
> (Bruno 2014: 19)

For Böhme, atmosphere is a fundamental concept of aesthetics. Atmospheres are made to work through "work" on an object, including interior design, stage setting, advertising, as well as sound engineering. These forms of work all contribute to the "aestheticization of reality" (Böhme 1993: 123). In other words, atmosphere is "'tinctured' through the presence of things, of persons or environmental constellations, that is, through their ecstasies." Atmosphere "proceeds from and is created by things, persons of their constellations." It stands in between objectivity and subjectivity. While atmosphere, indeed, can be felt as if it were "something thinglike," it is nearly impossible to make it visible or objectify its presence (Böhme 1993: 122). It makes sense then that the term "atmosphere," in English, can be traced back to the modern Latin *atmosphaera*, which, in turn, comes from Greek *atmos*, meaning vapor, and *sphaira*, meaning ball or globe. It is the presence of some kind of invisible entity within a specific space.

The significance of "atmosphere" is rather important for the study of techno-religious spatiality, especially as it redraws the relationship that is often assumed between the individual and "environment" in studies of religious spatiality, particularly in technologically-advanced Christian worship spaces. There is, as Robbie Goh has noted, a certain spatial logic that is unique to "charismatic Protestantism." The achievement of such a logic, which runs counter to traditional Protestant liturgy's focus on the individual's relationship to God, is through an "alternative semiotics." This alternative semiotics is able to interweave the "private spiritual encounter" with "the mega," that is, the greatness of the church (in both the material sense and in the sense of the body of Christ).

Thus, contemporary multisite churches':

> ... liturgy and operations are accordingly geared towards the performance and reinforcement of the size of the corporate body. In terms of its

68 *(Atmo)sphere*

physical facilities, it favors large multipurpose auditoria which are ... entirely filled up (with sound, images, equipment, church personnel, and finally the growing body of the congregation itself) in the course of the church service.

(Goh 2008: 292)

According to Goh, the achievement of such a spatial logic is rooted in the "principle of projection or proportion" (Goh 2008: 297). By this, he means that its success depends on the "imaginative participation of the individual" facilitated by the various technologies and design elements of the worship spaces as they "function at least in part to draw the worshiper's gaze and attention upward towards God" (Goh 2008: 298). Goh argues that this operates through a "multifarious" and technologically nuanced means of embodiment, which "[translates] the invisible and transcendent God into the body-sized signs and images which provide accessible cues for the human-participant" (Goh 2008: 301).

What Goh's point allows us to think about are the means by which a sphere, or spatial logic, is formed; namely, it highlights the importance of the sensorium. I draw from the conceptual definition of Charles Hirschkind, who approaches "the question of the sensorium not from the side of the (modern) object and its impact on the possibilities of subjective experience, but rather from the perspective of a cultural practice through which the perceptual capacities of the subject are honed and, thus, through which the world those capacities inhabit is brought into being, rendered perceptible" (Hirschkind 2001: 624). Accordingly, "capacities of aesthetic appreciation" structure sensory experiences.

Therefore, we can say that the successful achievement of a spatial logic is reliant upon the ability of media technologies to "activate" certain affective capacities of its audience vis-à-vis perceptual experience. Bright Church, and other multisite churches, in their use of digital media in worship spaces, rely heavily on digital imagery in their attempts to elicit a decidedly aesthetic response in their worship experience. This is demonstrated in both the trade and scholarly literature. Ben Simpson of *Collide*, a magazine that focuses on media technologies geared towards Christians, writes:

[D]igital artwork can inspire and invoke the imagination, tapping the affective dimension of our humanity. Good art produces awe, opening up new realities heretofore unknown, including the reality of God. Awe is a sense of wonderment, an overwhelming recognition of deep and profound beauty, wherein the soul is not only moved to contemplation, but is drawn in by that which is beholden. When the Church gathers, we make God visible and thus create space for the faithful – and our companions with reservations about Christianity – to have an encounter with God. This encounter can bring about not only a cognitive response, but an affective response that captures the heart. Media that points to God can lead us not only into newfound understanding, but to fall in love.

(Simpson 2010)

(Atmo)sphere 69

Simpson's discussion of the affective dimension of the digital image, which he calls "digital artwork," only makes sense when there are no technical glitches. The technical smoothness of this sphere, from the music, lights, and visuals of praise time to the very end of the post-teaching video clip, must be unbroken or else the wonderment that the worshiper feels will be shattered. It is not simply about relaying a message but creating an orientation of the worshiper's affect to receive God. This can only occur through technical perfection. Indeed, MacAngus at Bright Church–New York informs me that a mantra among all of the worship pastors of all the Bright Church campuses is, "Excellence honors God and inspires others." The discourse of excellence is not particular to Bright Church but is found in the broader context of Christian technology magazines. For instance:

> In fact I would argue that all aesthetical endeavors within the context of a worship service should function to supplement God's word in focusing people toward the one true God. Therefore, striving for excellence in our employment of visual artistry is not only an aesthetic endeavor but a theological endeavor. As media enthusiast Mike Apple once told me, "Excellence is when media becomes a transparent aspect of the service and not the focal point." Just as the teacher should seek to get out of the way so that God can speak through him, media should be a vehicle through which God can be seen as beautiful ... Humanity's apprehension of aesthetics, and even its ability to create, are distinct ways God has chosen to reveal himself ... Ultimately, our motivation for excellence in artistic expression supersedes philosophy, is grounded in theology, and is expressed as worship.
> (Capps 2008)

Birgit Meyer suggests that religions "authorize particular traditions of looking, upon which the sensorial engagement between people and pictures is grounded, and through which pictures may (or are deliberately denied to) assume a particular sensuous presence and mediate what remains invisible to the eye" (Meyer 2010: 106). This is the gist of Hirschkind's argument but oriented, instead of to listening, to seeing. The larger point that Meyer is making regarding the use of religious images is that pictures become, not icons, but rather ways of "accessing" God "by inducing contemplation" (Meyer 2010: 114). With the widening use of new media technologies to enlarge and spread these images, there emerges a "haptic visuality," that is, "a sense of being touched by looking at a picture" – an "affective visceral, and emotional experience that is instigated by looking" (Meyer 2010: 122).

As the French sociologist Michel Maffesoli notes, we must start from the a priori that the image is fundamentally a medium, a transmitter. As such, "it does not pretend to exactitude or verisimilitude" but acts rather as a vector of communion, "a support, for other things." He explains:

> [T]he image is relative, in the sense that it does not pretend to the absolute and that it puts things into relation. It is this very relativism that

70   *(Atmo)sphere*

renders it suspect, since it does not allow the certainty, the security engendered by dogma, or even the good abstract reasoning that does not embarrass itself with factual, sensory, or emotional contingencies or other "frivolous" situations with which daily existence is filled.

(Maffesoli 1996a: 72–73)

In Maffesoli's formulation, the image "matters less for the message that it is supposed to carry than for the emotion it conveys" (Maffesoli 1996a: 74), a twist on the McLuhanian dictum of the medium being the message. For Maffesoli then, "communication" must be understood outside the cognitive/ linguistic realm of signs and symbols but rather in terms of *feeling*. Thus, in this sense, the image is orgiastic ("orge", pertaining to passion) and aesthetic ("aisthesis" in Greek, pertaining to the senses).

In its ability to create both aesthetic and orgiastic regimes of "feeling with," the image partakes in a cosmogony of sorts, constructing "a matrix in which all the elements of earthly data interact, resonate in concert, or correspond to each other in multiple ways and in a constant reversibility" (Maffesoli 1996a: 76). The image facilitates a global conception of relationality that, beyond the different separations of distinguishing thought, stresses the organicity of the whole and the complementarity of the different elements of this whole – a key feature of the social theory of design.

Maffesoli goes so far as to suggest that the "bonding" function of the image indicates the contamination of religiosity into all of social life (Maffesoli 1996a: 88). Sporting events, musical concerts, and opportunities for collective consumption such as the one in the US called "Black Friday" are all Durkheimian "collective effervescences," in which the basis of the shared sentiments and emotions are largely mediated through images. In the case of the latter, the four-letter word "SALE" (always in caps) no longer offers up the calculus of a cost-benefit analysis to the throng of shoppers on that Friday after the ritualized Romanesque gorging of American stomachs known as "Thanksgiving" of all things. (We Americans tend to appreciate this kind of irony.) "SALE" elicits not only a psychological response but a bodily one, calling up desire off the bench, where it is usually the sixth man, ready to get into the game, and join everyone else who is experiencing "retail therapy", as Carrie, the lead character in the famed television series *Sex and the City*,' put it so well. It is, as Maffesoli describes particularly well, like a "trance" transmitted through "affective contagion" (Maffesoli 1996a: 94).

I feel myself other, and with the other I participate in a joint emotion that may be explosive or gentle, brief or dragged out at length, but that in every instance is intense, translating a very strong tribal organicity and best expressing the pregnant import of an image, or of an ensemble of images, in a given social body.

(Maffesoli 1996a: 94)

(Atmo)sphere   71

"SALE," in this instance, does not have much semiotic value beyond its embodiment of the linkage, "that mysterious cement – nonlogical, nonrational," needed for the religious outpouring of energy that is the consumer culture experience in the United States.

No longer is this effervescence reserved for "proper" religious activities such as festivals, liturgies, and rituals, but has, as Maffesoli argues, spread into the quotidian. We can even speak, at least in this regard, of a "rebirth of homo religious," or even homo aestheticus.

> [T]he renaissance of a social individual and a society resting not on distinction from the other, nor any longer on a rational contract linking to the other, but rather on an empathy that makes me, with the other, a participant in a larger ensemble, contaminated all the way through by collective ideas, shared emotions, and images of all kinds.
>
> (Maffesoli 1996a: 91, emphasis added)

Here, "aesthetic" means something very specific. As opposed to its cloudy definition as something to do with how something looks, it is "that which makes [the viewing subject] feel the sentiments, sensations and emotions of others" (Maffesoli 1996a: 111). To return to Meyer for a bit, the "aesthetic" is not only the "capacity to perceive the world with their five senses and to interpret it through these perceptions" but is also what Kant refers to as the "sensus communis aestheticus." And it is the dual foci – on the one hand, the importance of sensory perception and, on the other, the social nature of aesthetics – that grounds her formulation of the power of religion, in particular charismatic, Pentecostal Christianity, which she refers to as "sensational forms" (Meyer 2010: 756).

Sensational forms of worship, then, are a result of a complex of technological, institutional, and spiritual forces, and shape religious content through the body by "subjecting" (that is, making them into subjects) it to certain ritual practices and feelings. These then "modulate," in the words of Meyer, the practitioners as worshipers.

Sensational forms are largely responsible for the holist feeling of the immanence of God in a designed atmosphere, constructed through the "distribution of the sensible," a phrase she draws from Jacques Rancière, who describes it as, "the system of self-evident facts of sense perception that simultaneously discloses the existence of something in common and the delimitations that define the respective parts and positions within it" (Meyer 2010: 754). This, in turn, creates a "community of sense," continuing "a particular experience of the world that involves horizontal links between people on the level of community, as well as vertical links to some higher force" (Meyer 2010: 755).

The question remains, however, how or what media or technology facilitates this community of sense? This allows us to return to Maffesoli, who locates this communal dynamic within the "efflorescence of images."

72 *(Atmo)sphere*

The efflorescence of images is at once cause and effect of this organicity: they are diverse and multiple, but, entering into correspondence or into resonance one with another, they create a unicity, a cohesion that envelops life and the representations of each and every one.

(Maffesoli 1996a: 94)

This "unicity," he goes on to assert, creates a community or what he calls more specifically "the communitarian (tribal, ethnic, identitarian)" dynamic (Maffesoli 1996a: 114). What is specific about the communitarian dynamic as opposed to "community," is its mode of subjectivization. The "communitarian" roots itself not through a voluntary act or rite of membership but through nonactivity, as exemplified in the experience of watching television or looking at the digital image of the projection screen in contemporary churches. Though many critics of spectacle like Debord write disparagingly about the "passivity" of the viewer, Maffesoli argues that nonactivity is not necessarily passive. Watching-with gives the experience of feeling-with. Maffesoli describes this as "immanent transcendence" whereby this nonactive, impassioned participation leads to "that which transcends individuals [the sacred or its equivalent] 'is made immanent' in the group, and is going, in the strongest sense of the word, to constitute a tribe, with the dependence upon others that this never fails to involve" (Maffesoli 1996a: 112). This kind of participation, Maffesoli concludes, is representative of a "new style of Eucharist" (Maffesoli 1996a: 112), a transfiguration in the Catholic sense if you will, of the body or spirit by the image.

The image "[remakes] the unity between 'corpus' (the body, industrialized product, commercialized product, local community) and 'spirit' (quality, sense of beauty, disinterested caring, pleasure in the sensual, stress on the nearby and neighboring)" (Maffesoli 1996a: 120). It enables the body to be transfigured, to take another dimension. Transfiguration brings the person into an invisible community to go "vibrate in unison" to assure the "function of 'copresence'" (Maffesoli 1996a: 113).

For the techno-religious sphere of Bright Church, and other worship spaces like it, the image is a crucial part of forging a dynamic copresence and unicity. As the bearer of not only a semiotic message but a cluster of feeling or atmosphere, the image is the link of the community of sensation that Meyer describes. Whereas Maffesoli was using religious language as metaphor for the immanent transcendence of mediated experience, I suggest that we can overturn the relationship underneath the figure of speech and apply it back to religious experience in contemporary worship spaces.

Conclusion

In this chapter, I explored the sphere of contemporary religious worship spaces by viewing them as (atmo)spheres, which constitute "environments of feeling" through the aesthetic and imagistic deployment of certain technologies.

I empirically examined this argument in an analysis of the worship experience at a campus of Bright Church, focusing on how the technologies impart a sense of connection and bonding with the pastor and other worshipers who are in distant locations through a formation of an "aesthetic environment." I concluded that the resulting environment of the technologized worship space points towards a larger shift in ideas around Christian worship toward "liturgical aesthetics," which emphasizes embodiment and affectivity that are specifically actualized by digital, especially visual, environments.

Note

1 Names have been changed.

4 The digital milieu

The socialization of religious experience in Church Online

Introduction

In 2004, the Pew Research Center released a report from its Internet and American Life Project entitled "Faith Online." The takeaway, or "data point," in the parlance of the Pew, was that: "64% of wired Americans have used the Internet for spiritual or religious purposes" (Hoover *et al.* 2004).

But what is meant by "spiritual and religious purposes"?

Upon reading the report closely, it is clear that one of the main analytic engines driving it is the "spiritual seeker" analytic, found in the works of sociologists of religion Wade Clark Roof and Robert Wuthnow, which points to the emergence of a new religious sensibility characterized by people browsing in hopes of a loosely constructed spirituality drawing from many different sources as opposed to a stable religious identity rooted in a singular religious tradition (Wuthnow 1998; Roof 2001). A key finding in this regard is that "the online faithful" – those whom the report designates as people who use the Internet for "religious and spiritual purposes" – do so for "*personal* spiritual matters more than for traditional religious functions or work related to their churches. But their faith activity online seems to augment their *already-strong commitments to their congregations*" (Hoover *et al.* 2004: iv, emphasis added).

However, the activities measured in the report betray a preconceived idea of what religious use of technologies looks like. The report's conception of "using the Internet" for religious purposes consists of the following categories, listed here in descending order of response size: (1) *personal* spiritual concerns, which includes prayer requests, downloading or listening to music, sending faith-related greeting cards, and using email for spiritual matters (55 percent) (2) *traditional institutional religion*, which includes getting ideas for celebration of holidays, looking for places where respondents can attend services, making donations to religious organizations or charities and using email to plan church meetings (36 percent) (3) online religious news-seeking (32 percent) (Hoover *et al.* 2004: 8).

Needless to say, these categories of religio-technological activities are restrictive. They are especially so because they do not take into consideration

The digital milieu 75

the entirety of what media scholars and analysts have referred to as "Web 2.0" or "social media" (see Han 2011). In looking at practices such as the forwarding of religious-themed emails, the report finds itself speaking back to a regime of online practices that are dated now but even at the time of its writing were. Moreover, the categorical distinctions made by the report assume that they do not bleed into one another. For instance, on Facebook, which I discuss in greater detail and context below, one's personal spiritual concerns could be pursued alongside one's institutional, religious activities. On Facebook or other social networks, a user could be sharing experiences that resonated with the past week's sermon on her church's Facebook page while also be updated on matters of women and Islam as a result of her having clicked "Like" on the page of Sisters in Islam, an organization that promotes women's rights in Malaysia. These are not mutually exclusive in the context of social networks, a sentiment which the report somewhat acknowledges. This is not so much a fault of the analytic leanings of Stewart Hoover and Lynn Schofield Clark, the authors of the report, but mostly because of the pace at which changes occur online. The entire mode of sociality on the Web, not just for religious purposes but in general, has changed.

Hence, the Pew report does not consider the liturgical possibilities of religious Internet-use. This is especially unusual since much of the first wave of the religion and Internet studies were focused on this very issue – everything from neopagan séances in chat rooms to Muslim online recitation programs (Bunt 2003). Bright Church is among many churches that have, what are called, "Internet campuses" (Andron 2007). This phenomenon, it seems, would be outside the purview of the typology of the spiritual or religious use of the Internet laid out in Hoover and Clark's report.

The Pew Report, with its delimited conception of the religious use of the Internet, shows itself to adhere to what Christopher Helland, one of the first to study the nexus of the Internet and religion, calls "religion online," as opposed to "online religion" (Helland 2000). While religion online conceives of the Web as simply another platform for religion to take place (untouched and unchanged by technology), online religion hints at the possibility of a new form of religiosity that is facilitated by the Web (Dawson and Cowan 2004a: 7). Though indeed the Web and religion may have initially had a merely instrumental relationship at first, it is clear that today, with the emergence of cyberchurches in virtual environments, such as Second Life, and the advent of online worship, something else is going on. Helland's distinction, an apt one for the time, framed much of the subsequent scholarly and even not-so-scholarly investigation into religion and the Internet. But in light of the current media-technological regime, the categorical binary offered by Helland seems to be no longer tenable when looking at contemporary religious practices on the Web.

As Glenn Young has subsequently noted, there is clearly continuity between religion online and online religion (Young 2004). Young reads Helland's dichotomous typology as hinging upon a deeper axis – *information provision* and *religious participation*. Religion online, as Helland sees it, is

76 *The digital milieu*

merely a means by which religion gives information about itself. There is no aspect of religious participation (with some exception for prayer requests made via email). Online religion, however, primarily references its own environment, such as a virtual 3D environment, as the context of religious practice. This separation sits on a rather thin line, however, as Young notes, due to the architecture of participation of the Web, where linking is the hegemonic ethos; there is a "reciprocal flow of information." Many instances of religion online, like the website of the United Methodist Church, link to instances of online religion, such as Daily Devotional, a site that facilitates visitors' engagement in the ritual of prayer and reading scripture. Therefore, sites, such as the UMC's, offering a list of local churches, "further [emphasize] the connection the online world maintains with offline religious institutions and communities" (Young 2004: 103).

Religious community and communality

Among the many recent studies of new media and religion, it is Heidi Campbell's work that has arguably articulated the most comprehensive perspective. Drawing from methods and theories largely outside of religious studies (namely, science and technology studies and the sociology of technology), Campbell uses what she calls the "religious-social shaping approach" to contemporary media technologies (Campbell 2010). While her work is invaluable in setting an agenda for future research, a certain aporia slowly emerges around the issue of "community."

Specifically, for Campbell, "community" is the bridge that connects "the religious" with "the social." On this point, she is standing on the shoulders of giants. Classical social theory – by which the discipline of sociology largely means the writings of Karl Marx, Max Weber, and Emile Durkheim – can arguably be thought of as grappling with the dismantled hold of the Church, at least in the West, and its prescribed model for communal and social relations, rooted in systems of morality (Lemert 1999). The secular modern, then, is not merely a "story of subtraction" from the idea of God and His dominion, as Charles Taylor puts it (Taylor 2007: 560). It can also be thought of as the redefining of not only "religious community" but also "communality," that is, the nature of the social bond or relation itself.

To her credit, Campbell, in keeping with recent intellectual trends, does define "community" in large part through *practice* and relationships. Religious communities are, therefore, "groups who share a common ideology and theology and can be identified by distinctive patterns of practice and circulating discourse which support and justify their experience of the sacred and the everyday" (Campbell 2010: 9). While this definition is rather welcome as it attempts to avoid the pitfalls of some others that equate religion with faith or belief, there is, in my estimation, an undertheorizing of "communality," that is, the vicis-situdes of the relations that act as the glue for "community." In other words, if indeed the Internet is where these common practices are increasingly

The digital milieu 77

occurring, is there not a shaping of these "bonds" of communality by the technological environment in which these things are taking form?

There may be at least two reasons for this blind spot. In a previous work on the Internet and religion, Campbell suggests that the primary challenge of "computer-mediated communications" (CMC) to religion was in the realm of "community," especially the dominant, network-orientation of its social relations (Campbell 2004).

> Speaking of religious community as a social network can be problematic, as it appears to challenge theological and structural ideas of community. Social network analysis, which has been utilized to explain relationships and community structures online, describes communities in terms of net-worked, free-form relationships that are constantly changing and resist being tied down. Religious communities, however, typically characterized themselves as having a firm grounding in faith, in which community serves as a reflection of the character and likeness of the Divine.
>
> (Campbell 2004: 82)

In addition to the point about the incongruity of religious community and social networks, Campbell states rather baldly that what she is "most inter-ested in is 'official religion,' or religion that is practiced in distinctive com-munities where people have some sort of institutional or structural boundaries which define their relationships and process of meaning-making" (Campbell 2010: 8). Thus, the other approaches to the study of religion in recent years – "lived religion" and "implicit religion" – are ill-suited for her religious-social approach as it does not explicitly focus on the ways in which a specific *"faith community"* (Campbell 2010: 7, emphasis added) responds and reacts to new media. Implied here, then, is that "lived religion" and "implicit religion" are analytically distinct from "official religion."

However, what if, as the present chapter goes on to suggest, media-technological use, especially the World Wide Web and social media, by evangelical American Christianity, the religious "collective" analyzed here, demonstrates both signs of "official religion" ("belief practices tied to a recognized religious institution or faith community") *and* "lived religion" ("how people perform their religious beliefs on a daily basis")?

Therefore, the aim of this chapter is to suggest that there are new modes of communality that are apparent when viewing contemporary religious practice, especially in the context of technologically savvy evangelical Christianity in America. I will suggest that contemporary Christian churches that utilize the Internet have combined the logics of "online religion" and "religion online" in order to form a milieu that features not only the coexistence of religious participation and sociality but their *structural* coincidence. Put more illustra-tively, I suggest that the church lobby, traditionally where the fellowship occurs, and the church sanctuary, traditionally where worship occurs, are both "remediated," that is, paid homage to, rivaled, and refashioned in new

78   *The digital milieu*

media. I do so by focusing again on the workings of Bright Church, both its "Church Online," a specific web space where worship happens strictly over the Internet, and its Facebook page. I argue that the phenomenon of online Christianity is pushing religious experience and religious community, up to now distinct analytics of contemporary religious studies, closer together by facilitating certain modes of connectivity and communality intrinsic to digital media. Drawing from Nick Couldry's "liveness" and Michel Maffesoli's theory of "proxemics," I label this the "socialization of religious participation."

I begin first by giving some background on Bright Church and providing a phenomenological description of its Church Online, taking pains to thoroughly describe the workings and functionality of the GUI (Graphical User Interface) as it operates within the context of a typical worship experience. I do so following loosely the methodological and theoretical tradition of media studies, in particular media archaeology, which maintains the importance of looking at the formal aspects of media technologies in order to ascertain their social and practical impact on end-users (Gitelman 2000; Kittler 1999; Parikka 2012; Zielinski 2008). I then shift gears to analyze the ways in which Bright Church leverages Facebook, highlighting the particular character and quality of the interactions that occur there. In the final section of the chapter, I tease out some of the theoretical and conceptual ramifications of this performance of Christianity online.

Bright Church and church online

There have been many other attempts at church online. Bright Church was not the first. In fact, there was the Church of Fools, which was the world's first 3D, interactive church as well as its descendent St. Pixels (Jenkins 2008). What distinguishes Bright Church's Church Online from prior attempts at conducting online worship services is the GUI. At the heart of it is the video player that functions as a broadcaster. It looks like the video-playing frames found on YouTube and other video hosting sites, though what is missing is the play button. The video plays automatically during "experience" – Bright Church's term for worship service – times. Directly beneath that is a "Live Prayer" button that, when clicked on, opens up a pop-up dialog box that allows the users either to live chat with a member of the Prayer Staff or leave a message to be responded via email. Underneath that is a box that provides informational text based on what is playing in the video player. This "modular information box" is crucial as its contents are constantly changing throughout the experience, and contributes to the "liveness" of the Church Online experience (Couldry 2004). (More on this later.) Beneath that is a clickable icon that reads "Do you want to tell someone about Church Online?" When clicking it, it transforms into a sharing dashboard much like those found on the side of news articles found on the Web with several shortcut links to link sharing and social networking sites such as Twitter.

The digital milieu 79

In addition to the video player, which takes up the left half of the page, there is a box on the right side with three tabs that allow the user to toggle back and forth between "Chat," "Map" and "Notes." Chat, as its subtitle says, allows users to "mix and mingle" with one another. This allows for worshipers to interact using aliases or real names. Interestingly, the chat contains an "experience captain," who "moderates" the chat and is designated in the chat section with "(captain)," or some variation, after their handle. The "Map" tab displays a map of the world with red dots representing where users are logged in from with a list of "countries currently online." Next to that is "Notes" where the user can find a modified version of the speaking notes that the pastor is working from.

When an experience starts, the chat, which is the default "home" tab, begins to fill up with participants. Beneath the chat window is a box where the user may enter her "nickname" to participate in the chat. A praise band, usually the one from Bright Church's main campus in the Plains, plays various worship songs. After fifteen to twenty minutes of praise time, there are a few announcements, with related links and information displayed in the box below. This usually includes an introductory clip acting as a FAQ about how to navigate the various functions of the Church Online page. How the various tabs work is explained here. Following this appears a person who in traditional liturgy would be considered the "presider." It is actually Anthony Neil, Bright Church's Online Pastor. This person serves as the guide for the experience. He makes some announcements, usually about what series the "teaching" (or sermon) falls under. It is also when he makes the announcement for donations to Bright Church. While this is occurring, in the modular information box under the video player, various links appear regarding projects that Bright Church is currently funding. Functionally, this is close to the "time of offering" in many Christian churches, where congregants place their alms into baskets or plates. Here, this is done through electronic transfer on one's debit or credit card, and the presider encourages the audience to click on the "Donate/Give" icon on the upper-right corner of the page. After this, there is a brief prayer giving thanks for the offering (mirroring "offline" liturgy).

Then, the sermon, or "teaching" as Bright Church calls it, begins. During the sermon, the user is able to stay in chat mode. As mentioned above, the chat usually contains an experience captain, whose task is to moderate the chat. However, this does not influence the conversation much. Their task is usually to minimize the presence of "trolls." In fact, there is very little "moderating" of the discussion in that sense.

It is difficult to really discuss a singular "topic" in any chat room, not just this one. Chat rooms are rather chaotic spaces where multiple conversations are happening at the same time and users can jump into any of them without necessarily feeling like they are "butting in." Conversations between two or more people can be discerned by the torrent of "@," the Twitter-style indicator of directing a message at certain persons that is used in a variety of spaces on the Web, not just chats but also in comment sections of blogs.

80 *The digital milieu*

As for what the conversations are about, many of them revolve around how certain people "came to Christ," a phrase which has taken on the status of meme in evangelical churches, signifying someone's "conversion" experience. As expected, there is a lot of asking about where people are located. (Undoubtedly, this curiosity about geography is encouraged by the "Maps" mode, which visually represents where different people in the chat are from in close to real-time.) Sometimes, the chats resemble what Nadia Miczek calls "written chat singing" (Miczek 2008). Many users type out the lyrics of the praise songs, as if they were singing along, something that they perhaps would have done, or at least been encouraged to do, had they been at worship experiences offline. At other times, specialized ASC-II art, of which emoticons such as :) are a subset, and lingo is used. A popular one is \o/ – a pictogram of a person holding their hands up. Worshipers also type "PG," which is shorthand for "Praise God," at various times. During the teaching, some users re-type what Gottschalk has just said for emphasis, which sometimes extends to an "AMEN!" Chat participants also use various portions of the teaching to initiate conversations in the chat. During one particular teaching on courage, for instance, when Gottschalk is describing a rather harrowing experience in which he had to ask God for strength, a participant stated: "This is so true. I remember when I was going through something like this."

However, the chats are not always so on point. In fact, much of the time, there is not really a singular topical thread. The chats mirror those of other chat rooms, consisting of micro-chats and side-conversations. When compared to offline worship, the chat *is* out of place. What I mean is that the chat component could be interpreted as a means by which Bright Church is trying to compensate for the absence of the traditional (offline, face-to-face) community-building during "fellowship hour," a time after the worship when worshipers gather to have coffee and mingle. This is usually the time and place where relationships are formed, where the pastor or ushers have an opportunity to approach new faces. (In fact, Bright Church's Church Online launched "Talk it Over," which is a chat room where worshipers of Church Online can go to mingle after the experience [Byers 2010b].)

In short, I want to say that the chat component of Bright Church's Church Online is a vital, even central, component of the worship experience of Church Online. It is akin to what the Internet theorist Clay Shirky calls a "two-channel experience" – a live conversation with a simultaneous and "overlapping real-time text conversation" (Shirky 2002). As he argues, this kind of interaction, which is also called "backchannel," operates on a very different idea of what chat and other social software are used for. Usually, chat or instant messaging is seen as a "replacement" for face-to-face meetings. However, when using it among people who are in the same physical location or, in the case of Bright Church's Church Online, "web space" (i.e. logged into Bright Church's Church Online), chat becomes something of a new experience.

As Shirky explains, group conversations are breeding grounds, usually for interruptions of one kind or another. It is difficult to maintain a single line of

The digital milieu 81

thought for an extended period of time. But, if there were no interruptions at all, there would be a good number of valuable insights lost since often the most noteworthy things are said during tangents. The chat allowed for participants "to add to the conversation without interrupting, and the group could pursue tangential material in the chat room while listening in the real room" (Shirky 2002). It is there to serve, according to Shirky, as an outlet to the natural inclination of humans to be chatty and interrupt. Church Online's chat component functions as "in-room chat," a back- (or side-) channel space for "unofficial" conversation.

For Bright Church, the calculation was clearly made to reorient the hierarchy of values found in traditional liturgy. Whereas the sermon is widely accepted as the core of Protestant (especially evangelical) liturgy, the chat becomes a structural equal in this case. In other words, judging from how much visual real estate it takes up on the web page itself, the chat, for the designers of Church Online, is as, if not more, important than the streamed sermon. Hence, one's ability to build connections by engaging in conversations (that range from the banal to extremely topical) becomes ultimately a "win" for the online pastoral staff at Bright Church. One observes that this "transvaluation of value" of sorts is carried through in the way in which Bright Church also operates on Facebook.

Bright Church and Facebook

Each of Bright Church's thirteen different physical campuses has a separate Facebook page, including Church Online. Its Facebook page has several tabs – Wall, Info, Events, Helpful Links, Other Pages, Video, and other collapsed tabs, including Discussion, which the user needs to hover her mouse over in order see. Much of where the action happens is on the Wall, which is the case with most Facebook interactions. Technically, anyone with a Facebook account can join the social milieu or network of Bright Church. All one needs to do is to click on the "Like" button that is on every Facebook page, which, as of this writing, over 28,800 people had done in the case of Church Online's Facebook page. Clicking "Like" gives one the ability to comment on the Wall and engage in discussions, though one can easily read and access the various resources on the "Helpful Links" and "Info" tabs without joining the Bright Church's Facebook group. This means that for those people who have elected to click "Like," whenever Bright Church posts a message, a video or just a short status update, it appears on the user's News Feed (usually the default page when one logs into Facebook), which shows posts, status updates, and shared media from all of the user's friends and "Liked" pages in reverse chronological order much in the way of Twitter. Further, any comment made on Bright Church's Facebook page by someone else also appears in the "News Feed."

There are various kinds of interactions on Bright Church's Church Online's Facebook wall. Miles Allen, the Online Community Pastor at Bright Church,

82 *The digital milieu*

initiates many of them. They range from reposts from the Bright Church's blog to discussion prompts that relate to the week's teaching – for instance, "All through out [sic] the Bible God has been for our neighbors. How can you show the love of God to the people who live on your street this weekend?" (Bright Church 2010). This particular post elicited many different kinds of responses. Many of them are cursory, sticking very closely to the question asked.

> Last year we gave a jar of m&ms to our neighbor that said Jesus loves you. Months later he told us we saved his life because he is diabetic and was unable to find anything with sugar in it to boost his blood sugar. He stumbled upon the m&m's bearing the Jesus loves you message ate them and recovered. You never know what a great impact a simple gesture done with faith will have.
>
> (Bright Church 2010)

> I've shoveled snow off the sidewalks for the elderly, brought their trash bins in for them, made them cookies, sent them encouraging cards, etc whenever prompted by God.
> Any suggestions? It's really hard to love my neighbors at this very moment! They have a late night house party that has been disrupting the noise level & parking in our quiet street … it's 2:45am and I can't believe it's still going on. Pray for me!
>
> (Bright Church 2010)

Others are initiated by worshipers, and are more so the kind of typical, everyday status update found all across Facebook.

> My car got totaled 2 weeks ago, and I live out in a rural area. It's almost impossible to attend church. This is a GOD send. To make it real to me, I need to hear God's word every day. Read it, sing it, all that. Thanks.

To this post, Neil, the Online Pastor for Bright Church, responded, "Sorry to hear about your car, but I am glad that you are connected with us. See you online!" (Bright Church n.d.).

Communality as proprioception

It comes as no surprise then that in an interview with a Christian technology magazine, Allen, Online Community Pastor at Bright Church, uses Twitter as an illustration of the ideal "community":

> It's a network of interpersonal relationships … What's cool about the Church is that when you talk about biblical community, it's then focused on the things the Bible tells us to do when we're getting together as the

The digital milieu 83

Church – the edification of believers, evangelism, fellowship, and discipleship. That can all happen as you communicate, as you gather, as you have presence, as you feed into each other. The Web is very relational now, and you can know people and be known through those media.

The whole point of Twitter is having a presence in someone's life in the everyday. Twitter and some of those micro-media formats give you the ability to be present in someone's life because you can see what is happening in the parts of their day that you wouldn't know unless you were actually present.

So what we'd like to see when we build community, what we'd like to see come out of that, is belonging – where people feel like they belong to something that brings value to their life and they can bring value to a community that feeds into each other with those relationships and those values is [sic] now possible online.

(McClellan 2009, emphasis added)

From Allen, we can extract some tenets of the understanding of "community" that dominate in the discourse of the proponents of online church. As he repeatedly notes, community is *relational*.

By relation, Allen means something close to "presence." Twitter obviously becomes a very important example. Twitter, and "status updates"[1] more generally, as technology writer Clive Thompson has noted, reflects a new mode of social media that produces what he calls a "sixth sense." Since Twitter, and other status-update-oriented social networking platforms, encourages frequent messages throughout the day, one develops a sense of his or her social network's schedule and overall personality. This occurs even on a very detailed level. "The power," writes Thompson, "is in the surprising effects that come from receiving thousands of pings from your posse."

When I see that my friend Misha is "waiting at Genius Bar to send my MacBook to the shop," that's not much information. But when I get such granular updates every day for a month, I know a lot more about her. And when my four closest friends and *worldmates* send me dozens of updates a week for five months, I begin to develop an almost telepathic awareness of the people most important to me.

It's like proprioception, your body's ability to know where your limbs are. That subliminal sense of orientation is crucial for coordination: It keeps you from accidentally bumping into objects, and it makes possible amazing feats of balance and dexterity.

Twitter and other constant-contact media create *social* proprioception. They give a group of people a sense of itself, making possible weird,

84   *The digital milieu*

fascinating feats of coordination… It's practically collectivist – you're creating a shared understanding larger than yourself.

(Thompson 2007, emphasis added)

Thompson's phenomenological description of the experience of contemporary sociality as proprioception illuminates why Allen cites Twitter as a type of "community" he wishes to strive for with the online endeavors of Bright Church. To me, it is clear that the social formations described by Thompson, sought after by Allen, and exemplified by Bright Church's Facebook page, create digital bonds through the facilitation of simultaneity and immediacy. It is a collective milieu formed by what media theorist Nick Couldry has called "liveness."

For Couldry, media that produce the effect of "liveness" are able to "guarantee a potential connection to shared social experience *as they are happening*" (Couldry 2004: 355, emphasis added). There are two kinds. On the one hand, there is "online liveness," referring to "social co-presence on a variety of scales from very small groups in chat rooms to huge international audiences from breaking news on major Websites, all made possible by the Internet as an underlying infrastructure" (Couldry 2004: 356). On the other hand, there is "group liveness." "The 'liveness' of a mobile group of friends who are in continuous contact via their mobile phones through calls and texting" differs in scale and character. While the former assumes an audience, that is, a "public" of passive non-participants, group liveness assumes interaction or "continuous mediation" through a communications infrastructure "whose entry points are themselves mobile (and therefore can be permanently open)" (Couldry 2004: 357). Bright Church, clearly, exhibits *both*. With its Church Online, Bright Church exhibits the logic of "online liveness," with a congregational "public" that emerges out of the centralized broadcasting of the videostream, lasting only the duration of the experience time. With its Facebook page, Bright Church embodies "group liveness," creating an environment of constant contact.

Whereas Campbell, as noted earlier, dichotomizes networked and traditional notions of community, it seems that the Christians who use the technology see it differently. In other words, people like Sitz, Neil, and Allen are not suggesting that their Church Online mirrors the community of coffee hours and bingo nights – the more traditional techniques of community building by religious institutions in the United States. "Community," in the case of Bright Church, is not based on the logic of membership.

The tension between community-as-*membership* and community-as-*network* is rooted in what I view as an overinvestment in faith (or belief) as the primary indicator of religious identity. Numerous scholars of religion have warned against this, most notably Asad. "The assumption that belief is a distinctive mental state characteristic of all religions" (Asad 1993: 48) is a "modern, privatized Christian one because and to the extent that it emphasizes the priority of belief as a state of mind rather than as constituting

The digital milieu 85

activity in the world" (Asad 1993: 47). While Campbell, like in this article, may have been addressing Christian religious communities in particular, as Asad notes, what constitutes a "Christian" is historically fluid.

> What the Christian believes today about God, life after death, the universe, is not what he believed a millennium ago. The medieval valorization of pain as the mode of participating in Christ's suffering contrasts sharply with the modern Catholic perception of pain as an evil to be fought against and overcome as Christ the Healer did. That difference is clearly related to the post-Enlightenment secularization of Western society and to the moral language which that society now authorizes.
>
> (Asad 1993: 46–47)

But in addition to the historical shifts in the contents of belief, there are also the changing contours of communality facilitated by contemporary Internet practice. As Paolo Apolito writes:

> the Web surfer never gives up his freedom of choice in a definitive community commitment to reciprocal recognition, whether it is to a group, a movement, or an association. Every time that he goes online, he confirms the community, in other words, each time, he has an option not to confirm the commitment that he has entered into. And so it can be hypothesized as a devotional double world: the world of choices that in some sense bind and constrain, though never in a definitive manner, offline, and the choices whereby capriciously and pleasantly it is possible to vary, repeatedly, even during the course of a single browse and even simultaneously, opening up numerous sites and interacting with numerous virtual realities.
>
> (Apolito 2005: 241)

The fluidity of the content of belief that Asad highlights, along with the liquid forms of communality that Apolito emphasizes, beckons the question: What does religious "community" look like when in fact the standards by which "community" was interpreted have changed quite drastically?

Sacramental communality of proxemics

To approach this question, it seems appropriate to go back to Durkheim, whose work on religious life is where most religion scholars in the social sciences start. What Durkheim offers is not so much a better or "truer" definition of religious community but an altogether different concept. In his theory of religion as with his social theory in general, Durkheim's chief conceptual tool, "conscience collective," which has the dual meaning in French of collective *consciousness* and collective *conscience*, sought to view religion as the grounds for social (or moral) action, not merely metaphysical speculation about the origin and place of the Universe or a system of belief. The way that he

86   *The digital milieu*

believed religion (and society) to construct such a duality of the collective was through a regime of representation via the constitution of an objective, collective reality that is confirmed and reinforced through ritual. The relationship of ritual and representation is of special significance for Durkheim. "Religious representations are collective representations that express collective realities," he writes, and "rituals are ways of acting that are generated only within assembled groups and are meant to stimulate and sustain or recreate certain mental states in these groups" (Durkheim 2001: 11, emphasis added).

The technological milieu of today's online churches attempts to bring rituals, or sacraments – "miniature, personal signs of God and God's grace in the world ... visible signs of God's invisible presence" (Beaudoin 2000: 74) – back in. Instead of it being based on morality (collective conscience) or perception (collective consciousness), the digital "collective" that is formed by the milieu of Bright Church, both its Church Online and its work on Facebook, contributes to the formation of social bonds rooted in a non-absolutist coefficient of belonging, to use the terminology of Maffesoli. As he says, "anyone can participate in a multitude of groups, while investing a not inconsiderable part of him or herself in each" (Maffesoli 1996c: 144).

These types of social configurations, which he argues is characteristic of post-modernity, are no longer rooted in tidy, contractual agreements (whether expressly so such as in actual contracts, or implicitly so such as in familial obligation) or even whole-hearted identification, as the sociological terms such as "conformity" and "reference group" would have it (see Merton 1938; Turner 1956).

In suggesting that social formations now crystallize through what in earlier times would be considered "mundane" moments of interaction such as those in cafes or at the bus stop, Maffesoli argues that this ambient form of solidarity is largely rooted in a collective experience of intimacy or closeness through emotion, affect, and feelings. This he calls "proxemics."

> Proxemics refers primarily to the foundation of a succession of "we's" which constitutes the very essence of all sociality ... [The] constitution of micro-groups, of the tribes which intersperse spatiality, arises as a result of a feeling of *belonging*, as a function of a specific *ethic* and within the framework of a communications *network*.
>
> (Maffesoli 1996c: 139)

As mentioned in the previous chapter, Maffesoli is quite sensitive to the ways in which media technologies present images, and especially what kind of emotional response they produce. In this case, he is less interested in either a specific emotion or a specific type of media (i.e., visual as opposed to audio media). Instead, he investigates how "sociality" itself is in large part both "communicational" (i.e., largely influenced by contemporary media technologies) and "religious" (i.e., it produces a certain kind of "collective emotion," or "effervescence" as Durkheim would have it).

The digital milieu   87

Interestingly, he relates the experience of this emotional collectivism, which he labels, "puissance" to the Heideggerian *Mitsein* ("being-with") (Heidegger 2008) and places it in a genealogy of "mystical sensibilities" (Maffesoli 1996c: 24), which begins with Meister Eckhart, arguably the most iconic of Christian mystics, who stressed an experience of "union" with God (Kieckhefer 1978). Maffesoli evokes this tradition of mysticism when detailing the rituals of proxemics, going so far as to use the very word "religion" to describe this kind of collective feeling (though he stipulates that "it is less a content, which is the realm of faith, than a container, that is, a common matrix" [Maffesoli 1996c: 38]).

For Maffesoli, proxemics also approximates the Christian concept of the "Communion of Saints," which he rightly points out "is primarily based on the idea of *participation*, correspondence and analogy, notions which seem perfectly appropriate for analyzing social movements that cannot be reduced to their rationalist and functional dimensions" (Maffesoli 1996c: 40, emphasis added).[2] The affective-sacramental virtual geographies of participation found on Facebook, and social media more broadly, are precisely what churches with an online campus such as Bright Church aim to take advantage of. It is no wonder that Maffesoli spends much time on the kind of organizational mode of which he speaks, taking pains to give a plethora of synonyms – "networks," "sect" (Troeltsch), "polycentric nebulae," "communicational matrix" – all of which evoke a religio-technological register.

Mapping Maffesoli onto Bright Church's digital milieu, we can say that the "virtual geographies of social networks" found in its Church Online and Facebook page are indicative of a religio-technological proxemics based on shared connections of feeling (Maffesoli 1996c: 75), which are temporary, casual, "ephemeral and localized" while still being meaningful. It is the formation of a community rooted in the ritual of everyday sociality, such as "sitting in the café [or] eating a meal." These mundane rituals are "[confirmations], expressed countless times, of the link between the divine, the social whole and proximity" (Maffesoli 1996c: 25).

In true Durkheimian fashion, the "deity," in Maffesoli's analysis of contemporary social formations, is "the social," but for members of Bright Church's Church Online and the users of its Facebook page, the deity is very much still God. But beyond this difference, which admittedly is not by any means minor, in both, there is a collapse, or folding into one another of the religious and the social. The experience of worship exhibited in Bright Church's Church Online is very much that of sociality itself. By logging onto Facebook, as one would do normally, and seeing status updates of old high school, college, and work friends that read something like, "Finally, the baby and husband both asleep," or even candid photos of the weddings of nieces and nephews, alongside posts and updates from Bright Church's Facebook page, with its lively discussions of the week's teaching or a separate thread on a certain short video clip posted about a recent disaster zone that Bright Church is donating to, or even the frank meditations on a certain crisis of

88 *The digital milieu*

faith by someone, religious experience becomes woven into one of the many already existing technological sacraments of the World Wide Web.

Conclusion

To be sure, what I have thus far presented may not be interpreted the same way by the institutions and people I have described. In fact, the concluding positions that I have taken differ somewhat from Tim Hutchings, who has studied online worship rather closely as well. While we nearly agree on all "empirical" matters and, most importantly, on the "networked collectivist" sociality exhibited by online Christianity, I do not, however, perceive, as he does, a disappointment or "frustration," on the part of church leadership and congregants from the inability of church online and other kinds of Internet worship to "generate long-term, stable, committed, communities" (Hutchings 2012: 220). This may or may not constitute what scholars at times dismissively refer to as "an empirical question," although it is, perhaps, a matter of what certain congregants or church leaders have said to us individually; or, how we interpreted what we were told. Nevertheless, from the data I have gathered, which mirror statements like that of Allen above, Bright Church seems rather amenable to the "proxemic" sociality of its present constitution.

Thus, over the course of this chapter, I have proposed that the lines separating religious experience and religious community are being redrawn and even collapsing into one another in the case of a particular instance of the convergence of religion and new media. This, I argue, is due to the proliferation of a non-identitarian, affective mode of collectivity native to the "virtual geographies" of the contemporary World Wide Web.

While concerns within Christian circles abound (with essays entitled "Internet Campuses: A Blessing or Bogus?" [Out of Ur 2009] appearing in various parts of the Christian blogosphere), the socialization of religious experience does have a forebear in the small-group movement of American Protestantism. As sociologist of religion Robert Wuthnow observed in the 1990s:

> [T]he kind of community small groups create is quite different from the communities in which people have lived in the past. They are more *fluid* and more concerned with the individual's *emotional* state. The vast majority of small-group members also say their sense of the sacred has been profoundly influenced by their participation. But small groups are not simply drawing people back to the God of their fathers and mothers. They are dramatically changing the way God is understood. *God is now less of an external authority and more of an internal presence.* The sacred becomes more personal, but in the process also more manageable, more serviceable in meeting individual needs, and more a feature of *group processes themselves.* Support groups are thus effecting changes that have

The digital milieu 89

both salutary and worrisome consequences. They supply community and revitalize the sacred.

(Wuthnow 1993: 1237, emphasis added)

For Wuthnow, the proliferation of small groups – groups that find their raison d'etre beyond the walls of the physical structure of any singular religious institution – brought forth a changed understanding of "community" as well as, and this is indeed the larger point, a redefinition of "God." If the consequences of the digital proxemics of online Christianity mirror those of the small-group movement, then is there not also reason to suspect that the idea, specifically the internal-external (or more philosophically, immanent-transcendent) nature, of God must also be rethought? And thus, could we not say that with the socialization of religious experience, we are witnessing, in the formation of the digital milieu of online religion, the collapse of the sacred into the social?

Notes

1 Updating your status in a social media context is about letting members of your social network know what you are doing. This is the case not only for Twitter, which asks, "What's happening" atop its text box, but also for Facebook, MySpace and also instant message applications like AOL Instant Messenger and Google Talk (more commonly referred to as GChat).
2 The Communion of Saints, as a theological concept, is founded upon the Pentecost, when the third entity of the Trinity, the Holy Spirit, revealed itself to the disciples, giving them the capacity to bear such spiritual fruit as speaking in tongues. It serves, in many ways, as a precursor to the Pauline expression of the Universal as it allows for a loose network of believers to exist as a "community" by mere participation.

5 Is the return of religion the return of metaphysics? Or, the renewed spirit of capitalism

Introduction

The blurring of the lines between social and religious life, as noted at the end of the previous chapter, is a theme that has animated a great deal of recent work in the sociology of religion, especially the rallying cry for analyzing religious practice that occurs "outside of congregations (or other voluntary membership organizations)" (Bender *et al.* 2013: 8). As sociologists associated with this movement make note:

> [M]oving beyond congregations and other self-evidently religious organizations ultimately leads to stronger engagement with the "secular" or "postsecular" turn in recent theorization of religion. These approaches ask not only how the environment outside of religious institutions – both in the context of other secular institutions and outside of organizations altogether – "acts upon" religion or how religion "responds to" it but also how the very object of religion, along with its identities, authorities, powers, and constraints, is shaped through these dynamic interactions.
>
> (Bender *et al.* 2013: 10)

In solidarity with this movement in the sociology of religion, this chapter, in particular, engages religiosity beyond congregations with post-secular theory.

There is much talk today of the secular, secularism, and indeed the post-secular. Some critics have portrayed the uptick in discussions around secularity as negative – just another instance of an academic buzzword that is taking scholars, in this case, of religion and social theory, by storm. Soon the topic will fall by the wayside, along with other recent "post" terms, or so it is believed. But, in the context of this book, but also for the study of media, culture, and religion more generally, I stand by the importance of intellectually engaging with these "posts." While the sociologist Phillip Gorski warns us to "consider whether [their] growing deployment results...from a zealous need to detect epochal turning points in every minor twist of the historical road" (Gorski *et al.* 2012: 1), there is, he suggests, clearly still something to be learned from this "era of the posts."

Is the return of religion the return of metaphysics? 91

Of the many "post" terms, the one that had the most reach and effect is "post-modernism." This was the case because the debates around post-modernism began to make connections and build a larger picture of what was clearly occurring to the modern project, whose "core" was "dying." Referring to a whole host of aspects of modernity, including Fordist capitalism, truth, rationality and knowledge, European culture and Orientalism, Gorski suggests that the idea of the post-modern "is instructive for making sense of the post-secular" in two ways. On the one hand, some ideas around the post-modern suggest that we have entered a different era than that of modernity. On the other, some other ideas proclaim the end of "universalistic claims associated with modernity can no longer be sustained without demurral" (Gorski *et al.* 2012: 1). Undoubtedly then, secularism, foundational to the social, political, and even cultural experience of modernity, must also become subject to scrutiny.

Secularism's place of modernity has already been explored in earlier sections of this book, and has also been covered rather extensively by other scholars (Taylor 2007; Cox 1965). It would be unnecessary to restate those arguments, especially around the sociological concept of "secularization," especially since these were covered in earlier chapters. However, it may be helpful just to briefly begin with a detour into recent debates about contemporary secularism in order to establish its relationship to the concept of metaphysics. Metaphysics, I argue, is precisely the point of connection between the intellectual concerns of contemporary discussion around post-secularism and those of "post-modern" scholars of religion, especially those of a Derridean bent.[1] And thus, I see the recent efforts in understanding the post-secular as inevitably tied to the developments around post-modern, or post-metaphysical religion.

"Secularism," Talal Asad argues, "is a political doctrine [that] arose in modern Euro-America" (Asad 2003: 1). "The secular," in contradistinction, is an epistemic category, which derives from the institutionalization of secularism, mostly, according to Asad, through the formation of the modern nation-state and a particular regime of thoughts and practices that amount to a secular being-in-the-world. And indeed, perhaps the most important aspect of his argument is the demonstration that secularism is crucial in the construction of modern notions of citizenship. "It is an enactment by which a *political medium* (representation of citizenship) redefines and transcends particular and differentiating practices of the self that are articulated through class, gender and religion," he writes (Asad 2003: 5). In other words, the rise of the "capitalist nation-state" in the nineteenth century gave rise to widely agreed upon "principles of government" (*pace* Foucault), which were rooted in "a grammar of practices" stemming from a "discursive move" wherein a fixed understanding of human nature gives way to a notion of "a constituted 'normality'," allowing for "autonomous human agency" and, in turn, something like "the secular idea of moral progress" (Asad 2003: 24). The doctrine of secularism, therefore, produces the concept of the "secular," constructing a conception of the world – both natural and social. As Asad writes:

92 *Is the return of religion the return of metaphysics?*

> Responsibility is now held for events he or she was unaware of – or falsely
> conscious of. The domain in which acts of God (accidents) occur without
> human responsibility is increasingly restricted. Chance is now considered
> to be tamable. The world is disenchanted.
>
> (Asad 2003: 193)

Charles Taylor, in *A Secular Age* and other places, follows from Asad by
suggesting that the world of modernity is made up of "closed" or "horizontal"
world-structures whereas, in a prior time, there was the possibility of "vertical,"
or "transcendent" ones. The enchanted, vertical world had within it "nonhuman forces," extra-human agencies. Moreover, the line between "personal
agency" and "impersonal force" was not so clear in a closed world-structure.
Thus, meanings are not merely produced by human consciousness, to then be
imparted onto objects. But they can potentially impose meanings onto human
subjectivities. As Taylor writes, "in the enchanted world, the meaning is
already there in the object/agent, it is there quite independently of us; it would
be there even if we didn't exist" (Taylor 2007: 33).

Taylor sometimes refers to the distinction between enchanted and disenchanted worlds as having opposing "world structures" – one open and the
other closed. One may ask, open (or closed) to what? For Taylor, it is transcendence. An open world-structure reflects an interweaving of natural and
supernatural (Taylor 2003: 48). The transition to modernity, however, required
the elimination of this sort of world structure. The erosion, as he describes, of
"old views and loyalties" (Taylor 2003: 49) amounts to freeing "ourselves from
the thralldom of a false metaphysics" (Taylor 2003: 60). The closed world-
structure amounts to what Taylor calls an "underlying picture," which is not
fully conscious, "but which controls the way people think, argue, infer, and
make sense of things" (Taylor 2003: 49). The closed world-structure "naturalizes"
an image of the world revolving around an "exclusive humanism," wherein
"our political and moral life is focused on human ends: human welfare, human
rights, human flourishing, equality between human beings" (Taylor 2003: 58).
This is unique in human history.

But, "once you shift to the deconstructing point of view," Taylor writes,
"the CWS [closed world-structure] can no longer operate as such" (Taylor
2003: 51). This is so because deconstruction (or what Taylor keeps awkwardly
referring to as "the deconstructing point of view") attempts to unravel the
naturalized closed world-structure that secular modernity is founded upon. In
particular, it critiques the idea that modern secularity just appeared from
nowhere, and then permeated throughout the populace. Rather, what occurred
was a transformation of human identity as such (Taylor 2003: 52). With the
delimiting of human action within an imminent sphere of "this world," that
is, a disenchanted world, we become open to "the possibility that Western
modernity might be powered by...one constellation of such visions among
available others, rather than by the only viable set left after the old myths and
legends have been exploded" (Taylor 2003: 60). Taylor refers to this explosion

Is the return of religion the return of metaphysics? 93

as "the nova effect," where we begin to live in an "immanent frame" in which "religion" becomes an option among many. While religion itself can, and certainly does, remain, it becomes a truth among other truths. This, he writes, is characteristic of the pluralist structure of modern epistemology.

What Taylor describes is nothing less than what certain strains of social thought and philosophy have deemed "the critique of metaphysics." To understand the critique of metaphysics, or post-metaphysical philosophy, especially as intellectual context for post-secularism, we must go back to, as the philosopher Mark Wrathall argues, Heidegger, who first articulated a critique of modern metaphysics by deeming it rooted in "onto-theology." Metaphysics, put simply, attempts to explain the "being" of everything through, at once, "its essence or most universal trait" and the "ground or source of the totality of beings in some highest or divine entity" (Wrathall 2003: 2). Or, to put it in terms closer to Heidegger, Western metaphysics stems from the idea of "wholeness" or "totality," that is, "the unity of all beings" (Heidegger 2001: 68). The Being of beings, then, "both in the groundgiving unity of what is most general, what is indifferently valid everywhere" lines up with "the unity of the all that accounts for the ground." This, according to Heidegger, is akin to upholding the doctrine of Creation (Heidegger 2001: 69). Things cannot just be, there must be something animating it – either within the entity itself or some "ground," which may or may not be beneath the things in question. To that point, we can even look at the word that I just used – "animate." The term's roots stem from the Latin *anima*, which means "life" or "soul." The verb form *animare* translates "to instill with life." The notion that there is an external or transcendent being that is the author of such action suggests a Creator or some form of guarantor. Thus, metaphysics tends towards theology as it is basically a project "of sorting out the common properties of being as such (*to on he on*), of which God, as the Supreme being (*primum ens*) was the supreme instance and exemplification, on the one hand, and the theological project of establishing God (*theos*), as the first cause (*prima causa*) of all (other) beings, on the other hand" (Caputo 2001: 4).

It may be asked, in turn, what this may have to do with the contemporary era. Indeed, onto-theology may be the root of Greek, and then later Christian, metaphysics. What does it have to do with modernity or, for that matter, post-modernity? As Caputo mentions, the ontotheological project of metaphysics can be traced from:

> Aristotle's *Metaphysics*, where "first philosophy" has both an ontological and a theological moment [and] stretches through the great medieval Christian syntheses of Greek metaphysics with the biblical God, an idea that goes back to Philo Judaeus, and comes to a head in the metaphysical systems of "modernity," of Enlightenment scholasticism, whose illegitimate trespass beyond the limits of experience was criticized by Kant under the name of "ontotheologic."
>
> (Caputo 2001: 4)

94 *Is the return of religion the return of metaphysics?*

It was not Heidegger himself who was responsible for the wave of wrestling with metaphysics in contemporary continental philosophy but rather Jacques Derrida, who inherited Heidegger's anti-ontotheological project. What Derrida did was to give this a more pointed name – "the metaphysics of presence." By including "presence," Derrida cuts to the heart of the matter. Philosophy, after Plato and Aristotle, places a division between presence and absence, with the former having privilege at the cost of contingency and complexity. Derrida places this critique at the feet of Plato especially.

As an example of Platonic metaphysics, we can look at the concept of communication. As the communications scholar Walter Ong most famously analyzed, the *Phaedrus* is nothing short of the announcement of the inhumanity of writing. As Ong notes, Plato's disparaging writings affect not only human memory (if everything is written down, then we would no longer need to remember anything) but also the fact that, with writing, the presence of interlocutors is unnecessary. A text cannot defend itself and participate in dialogue. The give-and-take that occurs with two beings physically present cannot occur with writing, where the thoughts of one are interpreted, not fully communicated, by the other. There is potential for the reader to misconstrue the intent and meaning of the author. John Durham Peters characterizes this view of communication in the following manner: "Writing parodies live presence; it is inhuman, lacks interiority, destroys authentic dialogue, is impersonal, and cannot acknowledge the individuality of its interlocutors; and it is promiscuous in distribution" (Peters 2001: 47). Hence, in Western thought after Plato, presence is the condition of true "interpersonal communication as not only a happy mode of message exchange but, at its finest, the mutual salvation of souls in each other's love beneath the blessings of heaven" (Peters 2001: 45).

As we can see in the illustration just above, metaphysics upholds certain implicit conditions for truth and meaning based on something as abstract as "presence." Derrida attempted to demonstrate the arbitrariness of this preference. There is no evidence of why or how this is necessarily true. The notion that presence guarantees truth or high-fidelity communication or the preservation of meaning is simply an assumption and, thus, metaphysical.

While Derrida's work took off in the 1970s and subsequent decades, it was not until the 1990s that it became widely influential among scholars of religion, especially among those who were bridging theology and philosophy but also from other schools of thought. There may be many reasons for the sudden boom. Immediately, one must consider the influence and trendiness of Derridean thought in this era throughout the humanities and social sciences (see Cusset 2008). Perhaps more substantively, Derrida's influence can be traced to his own "ethical turn." Engaging in the work of Emmanuel Levinas and others, the "late-Derrida" explored themes such as responsibility, hospitality, forgiveness, and messianism, all of which had clear connections to religious thought. These are all worthy and acceptable explanations. However, I would maintain that the cross-pollination came from intellectual concerns

Is the return of religion the return of metaphysics? 95

within philosophy and theology regarding the limits of traditional (systematic) theology, which had inherited many of the metaphysical assumptions of modern philosophy.

An illustrative example here would be the work of Italian philosopher Gianni Vattimo, whose intellectual concerns in the 1980s and 1990s began with a critique of modernity through an engagement with Heidegger and Nietzsche and ended with writings on secularization. While a full investigation into Vattimo is unnecessary, a brief foray may be useful in detailing the connection that I'm driving at between the "projects" of post-metaphysical philosophy and post-secular thought.

For Vattimo, the "crisis of modernity" stems from a crisis in the status of knowledge. Following not only Lyotard but also Rorty and Gadamer, the relationship between the world and one's understanding of the world "does not function as a mirror" (Vattimo 2002: 28), he argues. This he calls "interpretation," which he summarizes in the following statement: "[T]here is no experience of truth that is not interpretative" (ibid.). Knowledge, in contemporary times, is not pure. Interpretation annihilates this prospect. The possibility of an "uninterested reflection of the real" is no longer; there are only "interested" approaches, which are all "historically mutable and culturally conditioned" (Vattimo 2002: 31). The crisis of modernity, in other words, is the crisis of the objective metaphysical bases of knowledge, "[culminating] in thinking that identifies the truth of Being with the calculable, measurable, and definitively manipulable object of techno-science" (Vattimo 1999: 30).

Yet, it is precisely this crack in the façade of technoscientific controllability that is responsible, argues Vattimo, for the "return of religion in our culture" (Vattimo 1999: 25). Technology, and the growing "production of commodities" that it elicits, along with the growing number of images across media, "[configures] the world as an artificial world, where one cannot distinguish between natural, basic needs and those induced and manipulated by advertisement" (Vattimo 1999: 31). Vattimo concludes that "there is no longer a measuring-stick to distinguish real from the 'invented'" (Vattimo 1999: 31). Hence, the basis of modern metaphysics is challenged, not only by philosophy, specifically epistemology, but also by "the techno-scientific world" (Vattimo 1999: 51).

But, to wit, the state of modern metaphysics, resulting from the development of technoscience, poses a "threat" to subjectivity, especially from a religious point of view. According to Vattimo, this is because materialism and consumerism has wrought a "Babel-like world, wherein different systems of values might interest and coexist." What makes the world this way is that truth or morality becomes "apparently impossible" to forge due to the "Babel of mass media" where "the play of interpretations" reigns supreme (Vattimo 1999: 52).

Similarly, John Caputo suggests, like Vattimo, that the development of science and technology amounts to a "case against modernity." Tackling this conceptually, he argues "advanced communication technologies actually undermine old-fashioned materialism," resulting in a world deprived of its "rigid fixity and dense and heavy substantiality" (Caputo 2001: 77). This, of course, is the

96 *Is the return of religion the return of metaphysics?*

language of Zygmunt Bauman and Marshall Berman, but also of Marx in *The Economic and Philosophic Manuscripts of 1844*.[2] Contemporary media technologies opened up space for "a new religious imagination...[T]he secular world became post-secular" (Caputo 2001: 78). But this new religious imagination was not the "return of religion" as traditionally understood. Instead, it was the return of "religion *without* religion." By this, he means something we have already addressed and detailed throughout the book, which is that "religious transcendence" takes on new and other forms, which create "an unmistakable tendency today to wrest religious phenomena free from the religions, to reproduce the structure of religion outside the traditional faiths and outside the classic oppositions of religion and science, body and soul, this world and the next" (Caputo 2001: 89). The end result is what he describes as "the amazing symbiosis of religion and technoscience in the post-secular world" (Caputo 2001: 71).

From Vattimo and Caputo, we can somewhat lurch forward by understanding the declining metaphysics of modernity as part of the "post-modern cultural condition." "Postmodern culture," as Terry Eagleton writes, "is depthless, anti-tragic, nonlinear, antinuminous, nonfoundational and antiuniversalist, suspicious of absolutes and averse to interiority." It is, in turn, "postreligious, as modernism most certainly is not" (Eagleton 2014: 188). What Vattimo and Caputo seem to add is that this shift is not only cultural but is necessitated by the blurring capacities of contemporary media technologies. It is not simply culture, an abstract term with very little analytic specificity, but specifically media and media culture. These dynamics have already been covered in greater empirical detail in prior sections of the book with regard to specific religious forms. However, we have not yet fully waded into what debates around "the post-secular" may mean for this development.

One of the principal starting points of the entire post-secular debate is the refusal of the "counter-secularization" label. Just as "post-modern" does not indicate a "counter-" or "anti-modern" stance, the post-secular is hardly a simple "resurgence of religion," to borrow the words of Jürgen Habermas, who is credited as the initiator of this discussion. First and foremost, for Habermas, we always begin from an "anthropocentric" position, whereby science and technology has already wrought a disenchanted, thus post-theological and post-metaphysical, world (Habermas 2008: 17). The post-secular is not a call to bring back theology or metaphysics, or even to "reenchant" the world but rather is an attempt at revising the "theory of secularization," which, in Habermas' estimation, betrayed "an imprecise use of the concepts of 'secularization' and modernization'" (Habermas 2008: 19). The post-secular, then, is not simply a theory about large-scale social transformation but one of correcting the record to reflect the current situation. To that point, Habermas ultimately summarizes the post-secular age as containing a "change in consciousness" regarding the role of religion in public life. Unlike the secular age, in which religion is relegated to the private sphere, so that it can stay there, never to be heard from again, the post-secular age affords "religious communities" a

Is the return of religion the return of metaphysics? 97

"seat" in the public life of societies (Habermas 2008: 19). The "post-secular," Habermas concludes, is a "revised reading of the secularization hypothesis," which modifies the predictive nature of its original instantiation (Habermas 2008: 20).

From this, we could simply conclude that Habermas' concept is not all that helpful. It is simply a neutering of the overzealous prophesies of the original secularization thesis. However, this is not necessarily true. As John D. Boy has written, Habermas' initial foray brought to light specific problematics that were taken up by other scholars. In particular, Boy points out that Habermas initiated the call for a "democratically enlightened common sense," which looked to push beyond the zero-sum game between "science and technology" on the one hand, and, on the other hand, "church and religion" (Boy 2011). In search of common ground, Habermas calls for believers to come to terms with reality, thus accepting and respecting scientific knowledge and the con-stitutional basis of politics. The state must engage with all voices, including religious ones. Boy characterizes this normative argument as one of *transla-tion*. All those who enter into the public sphere have an obligation to translate their ideas to terms that can be understood by all. This goes for not only the believers but also those who are not.

But, as Moberg, Granholm, and Nynas state, the concept of post-secularity developed by Habermas sits close to the general status quo of sociological theorizing regarding the "de-privatization" of religion. What this amounts to is "an increasing blurring of previously more clearly marked and differentiated 'secular' and 'religious' spheres" (Moberg *et al.* 2012: 4–5). To put a finer point to it, we can even coin a term after José Casanova, that of "reflexive secularity."

> Neither the naive, unreflexive secularity which accepted being without religion as the quasi-natural, modern condition, nor the secularist self-understanding which turned the particular process of European Christian secularization into a universal normative development for all of humanity are simply tenable, that is, can be simply taken for granted without questioning or reflexive elaboration anymore.
>
> (Casanova 2012: 41–42)

From these comments, we can extract, perhaps, something like "reflexive secularity" to describe the current situation. Unlike the unreflexive nature of the secularism of modernity, the post-secular age discloses a reflexivity about religion.

Thus far, we have forged a particular relationship between the post-secular and metaphysics that may require a bit of recapitulation here. We began by establishing secularism as a move away from metaphysics and also associated with the beginning of the decline of religion. However, many thinkers have suggested that there is a disconnect between the stated annihilation of the Enlightenment, for instance, and the actual state of religion in modernity.

98 *Is the return of religion the return of metaphysics?*

Therefore, figures such as Heidegger, and those after him, argued that there was a metaphysical remainder in the self-styled technoscientific, secular and rational, modern ethos. In a sense, we can say that the move away from metaphysics amounted to a secularization of secularism. Yet, there is a tension between the post-metaphysical position and the post-secular position. If the post-metaphysical position can be called a "secularization of modernity," then what should one make of the post-secular position that seems to "enchant" more spheres of life? As Craig Calhoun puts it, post-secularism "[signals] an end to taking it for granted that a clear, stable, and consistent demarcation has been established between secular and religious dimensions of life" (Calhoun 2012: 335).

Metaphysical capitalism

Then the question to ask is, How could these two intellectual streams coincide? It would be, unfruitful, I think, to only pursue overlaps or points of resonance between the two streams. There is, I submit, another, socio-historical reason, which is the increasingly metaphysical nature of contemporary capitalism. One of the key points of the post-secularism debate is regarding the increasingly plural "sources of religiosity." The argument that I am posing is that in the era of expanded transcendences and declined metaphysics, we have an increased movement of religious energy toward what Boltanski and Chiapello have called "the new spirit of capitalism" (Boltanski and Chiapello 2005). I rely on the analysis of Boltanski and Chiapello because the very shift in the nature of capitalism they present also falls around the same time as the discussions around metaphysics and secularism. If the crisis of modernity affected not only the place of metaphysics but also the secular, then it follows that capitalism is necessarily related to these developments.

As Boltanski and Chiapello note, capitalism did not start having a "spiritual" element beginning in the 1990s when debates about "the secular" raged. Max Weber has taught us as much. In his sociological classic *The Protestant Ethic and the Spirit of Capitalism,* Weber understood that capitalism is not only an objective economic system but also a value system that required a rational understanding of one's own worldly behavior. It was an intricate system of labor, valuation, and other market forces but also, rather crucially, a moral system of cultural values. Marx, in fact, describes the commodity as containing "metaphysical niceties." For Boltanski and Chiapello, what is specific to the "new spirit of capitalism" is its capacity to "[justify] people's commitment to capitalism, and which renders that commitment attractive" (Boltanski and Chiapello 2005: 162).

"Justification" bears a heavy analytic load for Boltanski and Chiapello. As they construct their argument, the "spirit" is seen as a "justificatory regime" for the individual's orientation to contemporary capitalism (Boltanski and Chiapello 2005: 167). Justification, put simply, is their word for explaining how one "invests" (psychologically, emotionally, intellectually) in capitalism

Is the return of religion the return of metaphysics? 99

and takes it on without much criticism. For those familiar with Weber, their method is similar to his *verstehen*. This "spirit" is expressed in three dimensions. The first dimension makes the involvement with capitalism "exciting" because capitalism is seen as helping a person grow, blossom, and even providing "liberation." The second form of expression appeals to the security of capitalism. Lastly, capitalism justifies itself by invoking a sense of fairness, "explaining how capitalism is coherent with a sense of justice, and how it contributes to the common good" (Boltanski and Chiapello 2005: 164).

Even though Boltanski and Chiapello call this the new spirit of capitalism, what is clear is that they mean something like "morality" or "ethics." However, that does not necessarily mean it cannot be described as metaphysical. Indeed, one could argue that liberation, security, and justice are all murky at best, and are "values," which most often tend to be rooted in a doctrinal system whether religious or secular. Again, we can look at the instructive example set forth by Weber's distinction between "this-worldly" and "other-worldly" asceticism. What is important to remember is that, for Weber, one was not necessarily less metaphysical than the other. To the contrary, at play was simply a shift in the *directionality* of the *certitudo salutis* (the certainty of salvation) and the uncertainty of God's predestination. Just as one was unsure of his or her fate in the afterlife, thus necessitating adherence to God's Word, there would be, in capitalism, an ethos of continual monetary accumulation as a guard against the uncertainty of the future – in *this* life.

Extending this Weberian line of analysis from Boltanski and Chiapello, sociologist Scott Lash has recently argued "the entire operation of capitalism, including the economic infrastructure is becoming metaphysical." By this, he means "that if in the national industrial age the principle of the physical was driver of the sphere of the metaphysical, that now the metaphysical principle infects the material base itself and is determinate in regard to the physical" (Lash 2007: 2). This could easily be read as just a rehashing of Marx as well as a reutilization of Bauman's "liquid modernity." (To this, I do not think Lash would protest too much.) But what marks Lash's comments is his equation of what he calls "intensive" properties of metaphysical capitalism and the "extensive" properties of physical capitalism. The latter, he argues, is rooted in an order made up of principles of law and equivalence. The former, however, maintains an order of, what he calls, "abstract inequivalence" (Lash 2007: 6). To explain this, he makes the comparison between "the physical capitalist commodity" with "the metaphysical brand." While a brand does indeed have tangible products, the brand in itself does not. "It is abstract." Apple and Nike, for instance, make products that assert a certain lifestyle, value-system, knowledge, and a host of other associations. The brand is closer to the fetish or a dream in its intangibility (Lash 2007: 6). The commodity, however, is "divisible into parts consisting of quantities of exchange-value" (Lash 2007: 7), most definitively that of labor-time. The commodity is not the only place we can view the metaphysical, or spiritual, elements of contemporary capitalism. In fact, many social thinkers have put this sort of argument forth in recent years.

100 *Is the return of religion the return of metaphysics?*

Specifically, Bernard Stiegler, the French philosopher, has written about what he has called the "spiritual misery" of contemporary capitalism. Writing in a similar vein as Boltanski and Chiapello, and influenced by Andre Gorz, Stiegler argues that we have "reached the exhaustion of desire" (Neyrat and Stiegler 2012: 10). "Today," he writes:

> We are living a third form of capitalism that is sometimes called finan-cialization, immaterial capitalism, or also "cognitive capitalism," "cul-tural capitalism," et cetera. It's what Boltanski and Chiapello call the "new spirit of capitalism." However, I think there is no "new spirit" of capitalism; I think that we are living in a capitalism that doesn't have a spirit, and that suffers from not having a spirit.
>
> (Neyrat and Stiegler 2012: 9)

It follows that one would ask what the condition of spiritual misery looks like, and how it reveals itself. It can be seen, according to Stiegler, by wide-spread disaffection. More specifically, capitalism, with its emphasis on calcu-lation, efficiency, and instrumental rationality, has stripped us of any sources of belief (Featherstone 2014: 9). In a word, we suffer from the effects of "disenchantment," which has "[destroyed] spirit" (Stiegler 2014: 5), bringing about what he calls "the fall of those metaphysical delusions that philosophy itself undermined by elaborating through the centuries, the spirit of critique, that is, of freedom" (Stiegler 2013: 4). But now, we are in "the age of generalized calculability, of secularization, of nihilism" wherein "God is dead" (Stiegler 2014: 4). This disenchantment, however, opened up the situation for capitalism to, in his words, "conquer the world." By this, he means that in the end what resulted was a "capitalism totally deprived of spirit." Stiegler calls this the "kingdom of ends" (Stiegler 2013: 5), whereby "every horizon of expectation, and of all belief, whether religious, political or libidinal...constituting as such that fabric of solidarities necessary for any society" has disappeared (Stiegler 2013: 6).

This has occurred mainly through a replacement of motivation with cog-nitive and affective saturation that is a part and parcel of media capitalism. The information overload inherent in today's capitalism promotes a "loss of knowledge and a confusion of minds" (Stiegler 2013: 87). In an argument that obviously draws from Marcuse's concept of "repressive desublimation," Stiegler argues that this saturation occurs through the constant solicitation of attention, especially that of children, by having their attention constantly bombarded to "industrial temporal objects...[diverting] their libido from their spontaneous love objects exclusively towards objects of consumption" (Stieg-ler 2013: 88). One could easily ask Stiegler how it is that the increase of affect leads to something like disaffection? Stiegler, again, draws upon Marcuse. We can see this in the comparison which Stiegler makes regarding the introduc-tion of automobiles. As he notes, the introduction of automobiles, originally intended to increase mobility and speed, has actually resulted in massive

Is the return of religion the return of metaphysics? 101

"immobility and urban paralysis" (Stiegler 2014: 57). According to one study, the traffic of Jakarta, for instance, has caused drivers to stop and start their cars 33,240 times a year. It ranks as the world's worst (Toppa 2015). Distances that could be just a handful of kilometers could take somewhere between thirty minutes to an hour, which I have personally experienced myself. All of this amounts to what Stiegler describes as a "cheap" substitute for enchantment. The parallels to Marcuse's analysis of the "happy consciousness" are clear. In *One-dimensional Man* (Marcuse 2002), as well as other writings, Marcuse argues that "advanced industrialized society" has, under the guise of convenience, created a situation whereby people are more and more dominated while feeling more and more liberated. Extending Freud's analysis in *Civilization and its Discontents*, Marcuse writes that "the Pleasure principle absorbs the Reality principle" (Marcuse 2002: 75). Ultimately, what results is a limiting of the range of possibilities for pleasure and satisfaction. Whereas desire, left untouched, is free to roam, thus attaching (or cathecting, in psychoanalytic parlance) itself to whatever sort of object. However, within the context described by Marcuse, desire and indeed satisfaction is channeled to specific, socially reproductive, objects and phenomena (Marcuse 2002: 79).

What concerns both he and Marcuse is the "substitutive logic" of domination in capitalism, especially at the level of desire or, libido, to use the word that Stiegler prefers. The void experienced by most in contemporary capitalism, which Stiegler refers to as "spiritual," is not necessarily one that has been occasioned by capital, but rather is almost transhistorical. As one critic of Stiegler puts it:

> It is a question that humans have resolved through the belief in various concepts. In ancient society, this was belief in forms; then under religious society, God; then after the death of God, progress, community, and each other; and then after the end of history, objects.
>
> (Featherstone 2014: 10)

These objects, no doubt "consumer objects," do not exist merely in the material plane. They are a part of a "libidinal economy at the heart of contemporary capitalism" (Stiegler 2014: 1). What is needed, now more than ever, is a reintroduction of motivations. This would be "the re-enchantment of the world," a "return to a context of associated milieus, and to reconstitute individuation as dialogic association and competition" (Stiegler 2014: 36).

Consumer spirituality

What is left unaddressed by Stiegler, but important for this book, is the possibility that there can be a substitution with some incorporation. Indeed, the sort of substitution that Stiegler speaks of, if the influence of Marcuse is any indication, is not a simple replacement. It is rather a filling of a void with something else but still that something else resembling, or having an affinity

102　*Is the return of religion the return of metaphysics?*

with, the "original." We can see this demonstrated most clearly in what is called "consumer spirituality."

According to some scholars, there is a "silent takeover" of what they deem "the religious" by contemporary capitalism through the discourse of "spirituality." Spirituality, in other words, has *taken the place* of religion due to the transformations of modernity, especially in the realm of social identity and affiliation (Carrette and King 2012: 59). The analysis, however, does not stop there. The critique goes on to state that the "contemporary use of" spirituality aids and abets "the social and economic policies" of neoliberalism, in particular privatization and corporatization of increasingly more spheres of life (Carrette and King 2012: 60).

Carrette and King argue rather strongly that we live in an era defined by not only consumer spirituality but *capitalist* spirituality. In making their critique in this way, they uphold, wittingly or not, a functionalist view of religion. "With the emergence of capitalist spirituality," they write, "we are seeing an attempted takeover of the cultural space traditionally inhabited by 'the religions' by a specific economic agenda." With economic logic "infiltrating" varied institutions such as "education, health-care, and professional expertise within society as a whole." This has resulted in the "erasure of the wider social and ethical concerns associated with religious traditions and communities." This economic agenda and logic is also, they say, not only replacing the religious with the economic but also replacing science "as the dominant mode of authoritative discourse within society" (Carrette and King 2012: 62).

Capitalist spirituality consists of an ethos of individualism and indeed "corporate-oriented pursuit of profit for its own sake" (Carrette and King 2012: 67). It is decidedly "post-modern" as is demonstrated by its grounding in information technologies and the "transfer of electronic data across national boundaries" (Carrette and King 2012: 67). Furthermore, capitalist spirituality shirks any sort of association with "traditional," by which I think they mean institutional religions. Instead, capitalist spirituality is founded upon eclecticism.

Although they do not state it in such a way, it is clear that the authors equate "capitalist" with ecumenicism, to put it positively, or promiscuity, to put it negatively, at least in the realm of religion. But one must ask what this means. If indeed being "eclectic" is then to be a consumer, and *inter alia* capitalist, then one must posit, in this logic, a stable entity called "religion," or rather a set of self-contained religions, which a religious consumer could participate in. In other words, the idea of "capitalist spirituality" assumes a supermarket of religions. To be eclectic would thus mean not to commit but rather to take a bite and move on to the next aisle.

Instead of this sort of moralizing, I would like to suggest that the supermarket is not simply a phenomenon representing the individualized greed of capitalism that has now infected the religious or spiritual realm. Rather, I want to suggest that it bears on the very question of the post-secular. Specifically, I wish to suggest that the interpenetration of contemporary capitalism

Is the return of religion the return of metaphysics? 103

and religion/spirituality can be thought of as "democratic commodification," to quote Bryan Turner (Turner 2012: 138). The alternative view of what Carrette and King call "a silent takeover" can be found by taking a look at the longer *durée* of postwar America. In this context, religion becomes a lifestyle choice, not an obligation. Protestant Christianity, in particular, by morphing into a mode of experience characterized by low commitment, individualism, and subjectivity, was adjusting to the reigning consumerism of the time. It is during the time of the 1950s and 1960s – the so-called American Century – that things such as "megachurches, drive-in confessionals, buy-a-prayer, religious films, religious shopping outlets, and the sale of amulets and other paraphernalia" began to take hold.

Post-war religiosity is not only capitalist spirituality, or *consumer* capitalist spirituality, but is also do-it-yourself religiosity, as Carrette and King point out. However, what distinguishes Turner's argument from theirs is that he suggests that this mode of religious experience is one that reflects larger shifts in modernity towards secularity, not simply the moral failures of believers (Turner 2012: 138). Thus, modern religious activity is organized around the same principles as consumer culture more broadly – "self-realization, personal autonomy, and emotional expressivity" (Turner 2012: 139). Religious activity has coalesced around the concept of "lifestyle" rather than doctrine. As much is clear in the technological strategies deployed by Bright Church, as discussed earlier.

For Turner, this amounts to "social secularization" (Turner 2012: 155). The adoption of commercial media and popular culture makes "religion ... fully available to the hoi polloi."

> In liberal global capitalism, the ineffable hierarchy of sacred beings is being eroded by a communication system that has democratizing consequences, and the religious becomes domesticated and tamed as the sacred becomes "effable." Perhaps one could even speak here of the emergence of the democratic ontology of the sacred.
>
> (Turner 2012: 139)

Contemporary spirituality in the context of capitalism is akin to "mobile religiosity," where "mobile people can...mix and match their religious or self-help needs without too much constraint from hierarchical authorities." We no longer have "conversions" but "brand loyalty," which, of course, is not all too loyal (Turner 2012: 153).

It would be quite understandable to ask whether the commodification of religion, as Turner calls it, brings about, as Moberg and Granholm write, "a general trivialization of religion and religious life and practice." By this, they note that the attitude of engagement with religion is "concomitant with consumer culture behavior," namely the latter's interpretive and dispositional tendencies (Moberg and Granholm 2012: 112). Moberg and Granholm think of this as the "relocation" of religion towards "increased general visibility of

104 *Is the return of religion the return of metaphysics?*

religion throughout Western social and cultural life" (Moberg and Granholm 2012: 113). In focusing on this "visibility," they make a very important point.

Visibility, to return to the debates around the post-secular, plays a very important role in the scholarship on the secular and post-secular. However, the question is not of *whether* religion is visible or not but rather how visibility as such is understood. Even Thomas Luckmann, who coined the term "invisible religion", understood it to mean that institutional forms of religion were becoming *less* visible. If that was his way of characterizing "the secular," then the "post-secular" could mean that, again, *institutional* forms of religion were making a comeback. Often associated with "the return of religion" are suspicions about religion's potential influence in the functioning of the nation-state (e.g., how religious identity may become an "alternative" to national identity among some self-radicalized Muslims in Europe). These are rather obvious tropes that come up in discussion around post-secularity and "visibility" that, in a sense, reveal the Casanovan argument regarding the publicity of traditional religions. What gets overlooked, however, is the changing nature of visibility. This is not only a methodological question of what interpretive tools are appropriate, but it is also a matter of theory, or ontology, that is, what counts as religion or religious. To look beyond the "conventional, instructional and established" definitions of religious phenomena is to broaden our understanding of religion but also at the same time honing in on concepts such as religious *expression* (Moberg and Granholm 2012: 114).

Immaterial labor

It is with this in mind that I return to the question of capitalist metaphysics.

I wish to take as a starting point a key concept within post-Marxist theory in recent years – immaterial labor. While expressly articulated by Maurizio Lazzarato in his essay of the same name, ideas and concepts associated with it have been contained in the works of Hardt and Negri, Franco Berardi (aka "Bifo"), and others. As has been noted already by many scholars, their work is rooted in an unorthodox reading of Marx, especially *The German Ideology* and the *Grundrisse*, about the nature of labor in advanced stages of capitalism. Berardi, for instance, has interpreted immaterial labor as not only labor becoming "intellectual" or "cognitive," that is, disembodied due to the increasingly digital nature of contemporary work in the wake of the so-called knowledge economy but, using a metaphysical term, putting *the soul* to work.

By this, Bifo is referring to what many theorists have already referred to as "real subsumption" where labor becomes extended to all sorts of social activity, not simply work. "The final point of this process," he writes, "is the subsumption of the productive labor of mental activity itself [as] the sphere of value-production" (Berardi 2009: 58). Thus, the "new economy" brings with it a new reality characterized by "info-production" wherein "no desire, no vitality" can take shape "outside the economic enterprise, outside of productive labor and business" (Berardi 2009: 96). In language that has influenced

Is the return of religion the return of metaphysics?   105

Stiegler, Berardi concludes that life becomes "destined" to production not only through work experienced as work but through "the constant mobilization of attention," affect and emotion through communications (Berardi 2009: 107).

As Alberto Toscano, a critic of contemporary Italian social thought, has analyzed, the notion of labor being immaterial was not something that came about with the rise of the information economy and "Toyotism" in the 1990s but earlier, with the advent of consumer culture and consumerism, which could be argued as already immaterial. The idea of consumer culture, and consumer capitalism, viewed "consumption" as not simply just the after-thought of production, but as an equally important aspect of capitalism. Consumption, in this argument, is not simply the buying of products. It is also the "consumption of ideas, affects and feelings." "The consumer," Toscano states, "is not just a passive terminus but a complicit and creative relay in the reproduction of capitalism" (Toscano 2007: 74).

To demonstrate this line of post-Marxist thought, Toscano points to the phenomenon of branding, particularly Nike. The athletic apparel company has one of the most recognizable logos in the world – the Swoosh. It also has the famous tag line "Just Do It." Nike, with its nearly universally recognizable brand, "[captures] the cooperation between brains" (Toscano 2007: 80). In describing the work of branding this way, Toscano is making the case for the aesthetic and affective elements of Nike and its products. In the words of one "emotional marketing expert," the appeal of Nike is attributable to a shift in focus from "product" to "attitude" or "lifestyle" (Newell 2011). Indeed, the phrase "Just Do It" can be seen as not simply a cliché for high-school coaches to cite in their pre-game speeches but it is also an orientation to the world that expresses precisely what Toscano calls "the incitement by capitalism of a simulacrum of self-valorization" (Toscano 2007: 80). Indeed, Nike, or any other athletic apparel company for that matter, hardly needs to extoll the virtues of its products. For that, there are thousands of athletes, ranging from high school to the professional level, who wear the company's gear via sponsorships. Nike's Air Jordan subsidiary, which, as the name betrays is headed by the former basketball star Michael Jordan, has gotten a lot of scrutiny for the violence that is associated with it as there have been many reported instances of robbery and burglary involving young people (men, usually) who are willing to, in some instances, even commit murder for these sneakers (Hill 2011). This is a type of incitement, which Toscano probably could not have imagined.

When speaking of brands today, it would be a mistake to not mention a brand that rivals, if not surpasses, Nike. This is of course Apple. No other brand, not even the aforementioned athletic apparel company, has elicited so much religious rhetoric, used to describe not only the devotion of the many Apple fans but also the figure most associated with the company, the late Steve Jobs.

On an episode of the *BBC* series *Secrets of the Superbrands*, a superfan of Apple named Alex gets an MRI done while being shown images of Apple

106 *Is the return of religion the return of metaphysics?*

products as well as other company's products. The host, having witnessed the ecstatic atmosphere and religious architecture of the Apple store in London located at Covent Garden, decides to explore this connection between religion and Apple. When shown the Apple products, as the expert on the program, Gemma Calvert of the Center for Neuroimaging Sciences, states, the electrical impulses to the brain change. This is most clear when looking at the orbito-frontal cortex. The change shows enhanced visual attention, indicative of loyalty. The brain scans are similar, she notes, to another set of MRI subjects when shown another set of images. These are religious subjects who are shown religious images. Apple has, she concludes, exploited the brain area specific to religion.

It turns out that the religious intensity with which people follow the company is not entirely by accident. Brett Robinson has tracked the religious ideas permeating all facets of Apple, beginning with its self-positioning vis-à-vis IBM. Jobs, he notes, wanted to counter the image of computers as machines for work. Apple's Macintosh computers, in Jobs' imagination, would be "spiritual liberators," helping to "[unleash] human creative potential" (Robinson 2013: 16). This is most evident in the famous television commercial aired in 1984 based on equal parts Plato and Orwell. The advertisement portrayed Apple as the lone hero taking down the idol of drudgery computing (IBM) and freeing the people from their enslavement. Indeed, we can see emancipation as a theme in the very name and logo of the company itself – Apple. They both refer to the story of the Garden of Eden and the Tree of Life. The logo is of course an apple with a bite taken out of it. "Knowledge, in the Apple gospel," Robinson says, "doesn't bring about a downfall, but instead provides a moment of liberation, a path to enlightenment" (O'Brien 2013).

There are more recent examples of this as well. When the first generation of the iPhone was released the name used to refer to it by much of the tech news websites was the "Jesus phone" (Robinson 2013: 60). The print campaign consisted of an image of the illuminated screen of the phone with a finger ready to touch it in a dark background. The tagline was "Touching is believing" (Robinson 2013: 64). This too has religious, specifically Christian, connotations. Robinson focuses on the similarity to the ceiling of the Sistine Chapel depicting the moment of creation, with the touching of God's finger to Adam's. While Robinson's analysis dwells on the Old Testament, I think that the ad also opens up a New Testament interpretation, especially of the days following the Resurrection. Jesus encounters Mary Magdalene and says to her, in the Latin version, "Noli me tangere," which means, "Do not touch me." This scene has become the subject of many paintings, the most famous of which is that by Correggio. But it is not *this* particular scene that I wish to center my reading on but rather a meeting between Jesus and Thomas, which occurs after this encounter with Mary Magdalene and after Jesus had made himself known to some of the other disciplines. When Thomas could hardly believe his peers, he had to see and, as it is written, touch the wounds of Jesus in order to believe that he had been resurrected. For doubting Thomas as well as for us iPhone users, touching *was* believing.

Is the return of religion the return of metaphysics? 107

Apple and Nike reflect the increasing centrality of the consumption of metaphysical qualities, such as affect, ideas and feelings, in addition to physical entities, in contemporary capitalism. In the case of Apple, what is consumed is enlightened liberation. For Nike, it is confidence. The brand, therefore, elicits a devotional practice that could be considered spiritual. It is the foundation of contemporary capitalist metaphysics.

Conclusion

In this chapter, I took the significance of conceptual contributions from the recent sociology of religion, including the analytics "lived religion" and "everyday religion," regarding the diffusion of religious life to other areas of culture, to bear squarely on questions raised by deconstruction, and allied thinkers, in prior decades regarding religion outside of the bounds of religion, which Bender et al. call "religion on the edge" (Bender et al. 2013). By tying together earlier discussions of contemporary digital religiosity with the larger question of "religion without religion," I brought to bear these resonant points with parallel developments in critical social theory regarding secularity and post-secularity. In assessing the major statements in the recent "post-secular" debates alongside current developments in Italian post-Marxist theory and continental philosophy around consumer culture and spirituality, this chapter argued that living in a post-secular age can also mean living amid the "return" of metaphysics, under the regime of consumer capitalist spirituality.

Notes

1 I must say straight away that I use the term "post-modernism" with reservations. First, I do not believe that it is the clearest of designations for a mode of thinking, a philosophical approach, a method, etc. However, it is the term that John Caputo, whose thought I engage with throughout the chapter, uses to describe his own project, which is a mixture of Derridean deconstruction, hermeneutics, and theology.
2 Bauman and Berman both take Marx's dictum "all that is solid melts into air" seriously and provide diagnostic analyses of modernity centered around the central figure of "liquidity" for Bauman and "ethereality" for Berman.

Concluding thoughts
Reconsidering "the sacred"

One of the major themes throughout this book has been the vanishing distinguishability of religiosity and everyday life, and the importance of specific deployments of digital technologies in this regard. In the previous chapters, I covered how these resultant technological spheres affect the fundamentals of Protestant Christianity, in particular religious experience and community, and also explored the possibility of the increasingly "religious," or metaphysical, form of life in post-secular, contemporary capitalism. It is along these lines, I would argue, that the sociologist of religion Thomas Luckmann wrote that "the religious" was in fact expanding while transcendence, capital-T Transcendence, long held as the universal basis of "religious experience," was in decline.

The vanishing distinguishability of religiosity and everyday technological practice demarcates not only the ways in which digitization affects the fundamentals of Protestant Christianity but also how technological practice reasserts what the sociologist of religion, Thomas Luckmann, once deemed, "minimal transcendences" (Luckmann 1990: 129). In "Shrinking Transcendence, Expanding Religion?" he argues that religion may in fact be expanding while transcendence, capital-T Transcendence, long held as the universal basis of "religious experience," was on the decline.

> [T]he socially constructed cultural models that shape the prevailing subjective orientations in the modern Western world – and, perhaps, in all modern societies – may be called religious without overly expanding the meaning of that term. I will suggest that modern consciousness, too, not only archaic or traditional consciousness, is concerned with certain kinds of transcendence.
>
> (Luckmann 1990: 127)

In pursuing this expansion of the term "religious," he argues that the decline of religious institutions, a fact often cited by proponents of the secularization thesis, does not in the least mean the end of religion itself. Luckmann calls for a reconsideration of not only religious experience but the categorical usefulness of the term "religion," preferring "sacred" or "sacred cosmos" in

Concluding thoughts 109

its stead. Luckmann points to the proliferation of religiosity or, perhaps more suited to his terminology, the diffusion of transcendences in the use of "the sacred." This of course has implications for how "the cosmos" is conceived. Luckmann again:

> The "sacred cosmos" of modern industrial societies no longer has one obligatory hierarchy, and it is no longer articulated as a consistent thematic whole. It consists of assortments of social reconstructions of transcendence. The term "assortment" points out a significant distinction between the modern sacred cosmos and the sacred cosmos of a traditional society. The latter contains well-articulated themes that form a universe of "ultimate" significance that is reasonably consistent in terms of its own logic ... [Today] these themes, however, do not form a coherent universe. The assortment of religious representations – a sacred cosmos in a loose sense of the term only – is not internalized by potential consumers as a whole...Individual religiosity is thus no longer a replica or approximation of an "official" model.
>
> (Luckmann 1990: 134)

In a 1978 essay called "The Return of the Sacred: The Argument about the Future of Religion," the sociologist and cultural critic Daniel Bell announced that Weber was right. In declaring that modernity had disenchanted the world, one of the founding fathers of sociology had rightly predicted that the world had become sapped of its mystery.

> With the progress of science and technology, man has stopped believing in magic powers, in spirits and demons: he has lost his sense of prophecy and, above all, his sense of the sacred. Reality has become dreary, flat and utilitarian, leaving a great void in the souls of men which they seek to fill by furious activity and through various devices and substitutes.
>
> (Bell 1978: 30)

As one could imagine, by making such a statement, Bell was putting forth a call to action as much as he was an argument. Bell, at this time, was well into his neo-conservative period. And, with this in mind, it is rather clear what kind of argument he is going to put forth. Influenced by Weber, he argued that so-called secularization actually meant the rise of two different kinds of phenomena – one social, the other cultural. These two sets were quite distinct and were incongruent with one another (Bell 1978: 31). Socially, secularization means that the institutional authority of religion over public life was shrinking. Religions, while they still have influence over their own followers, no longer exert power on others. Indeed, in places with constitutional provisions for the separation of church and state (such as in the United States) or laicite (such as in France), this kind of argument holds true. Bell states that this can be explained through "rationalization." If we understand

110 *Concluding thoughts*

it in the same way as Weber, then rationalization, as the process of placing the logic of calculation and efficiency at the core of all social processes, then indeed the separating out of religion from the public sphere can be seen as part and parcel of the process. Culturally, though, there is something else at play. As a result of the disenchanting of the world (which is, for Bell, separate from rationalization), the nihlist thread of modernity has taken over (Bell 1978: 32). To understand the full extent of Bell's argument, we have to see what he means by culture, and its relationship to religion.

Culture, for Bell, consists of the "modalities of response" to the culturally universal questions of death, tragedy, and love. In a strikingly existentialist tone, Bell argues that culture is a way of dealing with "the finiteness of existence" (Bell 1978: 33). Religion, likewise, consists of an attempt to deal with these existential questions. What makes it unique is its "codification" into creeds, rites, and institutions (Bell 1978: 34). However, since the ninetennth century, other cultural forms of pursuing answers to these existential questions took off. One of these "alternative responses" came from the expressive arts and what Bell, rather curiously, calls "aestheticism" and sometimes "Modernism" (Bell 1978: 40). It is from within this movement that Bell finds the deciding point of decline that spelled doom for religion's dominance in the "zero-sum game of man's expressive desires." Artistic modernism, by delinking the erotic from the religious, and thus "freeing all other norms of morality and rational conduct" from the erotic, wrought a period of decadence and hedonism, which eventually "abolished God" and ascribed to human beings the powers that were once reserved for God (Bell 1978: 45). This "profanation," as Bell calls it, has resulted in some dire consequences, the most significant of which is that "restraint has gone slack." In other words, the primal impulses (which for Bell are clearly Freudian as his examples of sexuality and violence demonstrate) are no longer properly "channeled into religion" and now are "polymorph [sic] perverse and pervade all dimensions of modern culture" (Bell 1978: 37). Moreover, Bell suggests that the profanation has been spurred by consumer culture. "What has been art," he writes, "becomes trendy life-style and what has been incorporation (as in transubstantiation) becomes consumption." Culture, today, is consumer culture, "with its demands for self-fulfillment" (Bell 1978: 47). As one critic of Bell writes:

> Bell's neo-conservative lament for the moral values of a solidary bourgeois society in which the bond of religion is strong and resilient enough to bear the creative tensions of bounded Protestantism and spirited capitalism. At bottom, Bell attributes the crisis of capitalism to a crisis of religion, to a loss of ultimate meaning which undercuts its civic will.
>
> (O'Neill 1988: 494)

It is precisely because of this crisis, at once in social order, in capitalism, and in culture, that Bell calls for the *renewal* of the sacred.

Concluding thoughts 111

But what exactly is the sacred for Bell?

> The sacred is the space of wonder and awe, of the noumenal which remains a mystery and the numinous which is its aura. With the sacred is the principle *Havdolah* [sic: *Havdalah*], the principle of distinction, of the realm which is reserved for the days of awe and lament, and the realm of the mundane and profane.
>
> (Bell 1978: 54)

Adopting the anthropological definition of the sacred, Bell argues that the principle of separation, indeed the actual meaning of *Havdalah*, is now lost. Everything is integrated. Bell attributes this profane integration to capitalism, which "treats nothing as sacred, but converts all objects into commodities to be bought and sold to the highest bidders" (Bell 1978: 55).

Leaving aside Bell's cultural conservatism, with which I share no sympathy, Bell's analysis is an occasion to consider whether capitalism, in particular consumer culture, is indeed somewhat responsible for "profanation" or abolishing the sacred. Indeed, the arguments presented in the prior chapter, which show a renewed spirit of contemporary capitalism, seem to refute such a claim. But this need not be a case of either/or.

We can follow the analysis of the theologian Graham Ward, who has recently argued that no matter what periodizing, diagnostic term we choose to label the current era, the changes to "modes of believing and the structure of sensibilities" is rather clear (Ward 2006: 182). In the Middle Ages, religion included "faith, piety, worship and the ethics and aesthetics of the Good and the Beautiful." Today, it includes "myth, spirituality, mystical experience, reenchantment, [and] holistic notions of health and self-help" (Ward 2006: 180). It is this shift that is primarily responsible for a "media-oriented consumer spirituality" (Ward 2006: 185). This media-oriented consumer spirituality feeds a desire to be entertained and, as Ward aptly says, "to live the designer life." This includes not only designer bags and shoes but also designer lifestyles.

> Now all and any specific religious tradition (whatever the tradition's geographical origins) can be branded and sold worldwide – Christian angels, Jewish kabbalah, the Hindu ars erotica, Confucian meditations, Haitian voodoo dolls, Islamic tiles, celtic blessings.
>
> (Ward 2006: 185)

For Ward, this results in the depoliticization of spirituality, not the moral decay of modern, bourgeois society. First, this sort of consumer spirituality atomizes individuals. It makes the religious tradition subject to the wants and needs of the individual without the requisite forming of a new self that is oriented towards the religious community. The aim of this type of spirituality is personal satisfaction. And to that point, consumer spirituality, second,

112   *Concluding thoughts*

"threatens" democratic participation. Not only is there no desire for community but there is no "critical engagement in public fora" (Ward 2006: 183). Ward's general pessimism about contemporary spirituality and its relationship to capitalism must be reckoned with. It is not unfounded, as the examples in the previous chapter about Apple and Nike make clear.

While both Ward and Bell are deeply concerned about the decline in the Durkheimian social bond, with Ward using the language of democracy and Bell referring to civic will, what distinguishes one from the other is their respective stances on the sacred and enchantment. For Bell, capitalism has had frightful consequences for culture. It has, in effect, cheapened it, making it into lifestyle, taking away its existential and universal qualities. One could see some sprinklings of the Frankfurt School in Bell, in particular the idea of the "totally administered society" as well as the general overarching cultural pessimism. But it seems that Bell could only handle one side of the dialectic presented by Critical Theory. The other side of total administration and one-dimensionality is of course the culture industry, which operates through the logic of the terms that Ward associates with contemporary spirituality – enchantment, mysticism, and experience. For Ward, capitalism has not eliminated the sacred but has revived it, and directed it toward consumer identity, consisting of a self that wishes to be entertained.

While their positions are similar regarding the loss of communal life, what may account for the difference is their respective understandings of the nature of contemporary subjectivity: As we can glean from his argument, Bell views the subject as defined by a drive toward not only meaning but a seamless, total worldview. Without it, there is crisis. That is why, for him, the subject is so easily swayed by the techniques of other "alternative responses" to the existential questions of life. Ward's subject, however, differs in that it no longer seeks a total worldview but rather smaller bits and pieces from which the subject can construct a lifestyle. There are only "alternatives" in the religio-cultural landscape of Ward. If the idea of the post-secular has any purchase, it is because of its mostly correct argument that "the secular certainties," as sociologist Grace Davie describes "science, rationalism, progress, etc.," are "themselves under attack." There are no longer any "erstwhile competitors of religious truth" that will stand as a "recognizable and unified religious alternative" (Davie 2004: 78).

The sacred today, against the hopes and wishes of Bell, is incoherent. It is, as Bronislaw Szersynski argues, "postmodern" and "global" (Szerszynski 2005). The monotheistic dualism that used to divide the sacred and the profane has given way to a "multiplex reality, one filled with and constituted by different cosmologies and world-views grounded in subjective experience" (Szerszynski 2005: 22). Neither religion nor science has a monopoly on how people view the world and themselves. To the contrary, in the post-modern and global sacred, "people feel obliged to fashion or choose religious and cosmological ideas on the basis of...what 'feels right' to them" (Szerszynski 2005: 22). The sacred is not transcendent. It does not prescribe meaning. As Szersynski notes, "consumer culture exploits this ambiguity of global images, completing the sign with its own, brand-specific signifiers" (Szerszynski 2005: 167). Perhaps we can say the sacred has returned but is no longer able to transcend in the way that Bell sought. The numinous has given way to the mundane, and the *noumenon* to the *phenomenon*. The contemporary ethos of digital culture, after all, is "pics or it didn't happen." According to Marcel Gauchet, the secularization of the sacred gave rise to religion in its rational form, with institutions, rites, and doctrines. In this media age, it seems that the secularization of religion has brought forth the return of metaphysics and the sacred, albeit in immanent form.

References

Albanese, C.L., 1981. *America: Religions and Religion*, Belmont, CA: Wadsworth Pub. Co.

Allcot, D., 2009. 'Worship Facilities Magazine Editorial.' *Worship Facilities Magazine.* Available at: www.worshipfacilities.com/go.php/editorial/8492 [Accessed May 7, 2010].

Alliez, É. and Sloterdijk, P., 2007. 'Living Hot, Thinking Coldly: An Interview with Peter Sloterdijk.' *Cultural Politics: An International Journal*, 3: 307–326.

Altizer, T.J.J. and Hamilton, W., 1966. *Radical Theology and the Death of God*, Indianapolis, IN: Bobbs-Merrill.

Ammerman, N.T., 1987. *Bible Believers: Fundamentalists in the Modern World*, New Brunswick, NJ: Rutgers University Press.

Ammerman, N.T. ed., 2007. *Everyday Religion: Observing Modern Religious Lives*, Oxford and New York: Oxford University Press.

Ammerman, N.T. and Farnsley, A.E., 1997. *Congregation & Community*, New Brunswick, NJ: Rutgers University Press.

Andron, S., 2007. 'Internet Churches and Religious Webcasts Drawing More Congregants.' *The Denver Post*. Available at: www.denverpost.com/technology/ci_7228105 [Accessed July 9, 2010].

Anon, 2013. 'The Percentage of the Population with No Religion Has Increased in England and Wales.' *Office for National Statistics*. Available at: www.ons.gov.uk/ons/interactive/census-map-2-1—religion/index.html?mode=clean [Accessed June 2, 2015].

Apolito, P., 2005. *The Internet and the Madonna: Religious Visionary Experience on the Web*, Chicago, IL: University of Chicago Press.

Armstrong, K., 2000. *Islam: A Short History*, New York: Modern Library.

Aronowitz, S., 1993. *Roll Over Beethoven: The Return of Cultural Strife*, Middletown, CT: Wesleyan University Press.

arXiv, 2014. 'How the Internet Is Taking Away America's Religion.' *MIT Technology Review*. Available at: www.technologyreview.com/view/526111/how-the-internet-is-taking-away-americas-religion [Accessed May 21, 2015].

Asad, T., 1993. *Genealogies of Religion: Discipline and Reasons of Power in Christianity and Islam*, Baltimore, MD: The Johns Hopkins University Press.

Asad, T., 2003. *Formations of the Secular: Christianity, Islam, Modernity*, Palo Alto, CA: Stanford University Press.

Badiou, A., 2009. *Saint Paul: The Foundation of Universalism*, Stanford, CA: Stanford University Press.

References 115

Barbour, I.G., 1966. *Issues in Science and Religion*, Englewood Cliffs, NJ: Prentice-Hall.

Barna Group, 2008. 'The Barna Group – New Research Describes Use of Technology in Churches.' Available at: www.barna.org/barna-update/article/14-media/40-new-research-describes-use-of-technology-in-churches [Accessed May 5, 2010].

Barnhart, R., 2008. 'Multi-Site Mishaps and Misconceptions.' *Collide Magazine*. Available at: www.collidemagazine.com/article/113/multi-site-mishaps-and-miscon ceptions [Accessed August 9, 2010].

Baudrillard, J., 1991. *Seduction*, English ed, New York: Palgrave Macmillan.

BBC News, 2010a. 'Costa Rica-Nicaragua border row.' *BBC*. Available at: www.bbc. co.uk/news/world-latin-america-11751727 [Accessed November 25, 2010].

BBC News, 2010b. 'Germans opt out of Google plans.' *BBC*. Available at: www.bbc. co.uk/news/technology-11595495 [Accessed November 25, 2010].

Beaudoin, T., 2000. *Virtual Faith: The Irreverent Spiritual Quest of Generation X*, San Francisco, CA: Wiley.

Beck, U., 2006. *The Cosmopolitan Vision*, Cambridge and Malden, MA: Polity.

Beck, U., Giddens, A., and Lash, S., 1994. *Reflexive Modernization: Politics, Tradition and Aesthetics in the Modern Social Order*, first edn, Palo Alto, CA: Stanford University Press.

Beckford, J.A., 1985. 'The Insulation and Isolation of the Sociology of Religion.' *Sociological Analysis*, 46(4): 347–354.

Bell, D., 1978. 'The Return of the Sacred: The Argument about the Future of Religion.' *Zygon*, 13(3): 187–208.

Bellah, R., 1964. 'Religious Evolution.' *American Sociological Review*, 29(3): 358–374.

Bellah, R.N., 1970. *Beyond Belief: Essays on Religion in a Post-traditional World*, New York: Harper & Row.

Bender, C., 2012. "Things in Their Entanglements." In P. Gorskiet *et al.*, eds, *The Post-Secular in Question: Religion in Contemporary Society*, New York: NYU Press: 43–76.

Bender, C., Cadge, W., Levitt, P., and Smilde, D., eds, 2013. *Religion on the Edge: De-centering and Re-centering the Sociology of Religion*, Oxford and New York: Oxford University Press.

Benedictus XVI, 2010. 'Message for the 44th World Communications Day.' *Vatican. va*. Available at: www.vatican.va/holy_father/benedict_xvi/messages/communica tions/documents/hf_ben-xvi_mes_20100124_44th-world-communications-day_en.html [Accessed January 27, 2011].

Benedictus XVI, 2011. 'Message for the 45th World Communications Day.' *Vatican. va*. Available at: www.vatican.va/holy_father/benedict_xvi/messages/communica tions/documents/hf_ben-xvi_mes_20110124_45th-world-communications-day_en.html [Accessed January 27, 2011].

Bennett, J., 2001. *The Enchantment of Modern Life: Attachments, Crossings, and Ethics*, Princeton, NJ: Princeton University Press.

Berardi, F., 2009. *The Soul at Work: From Alienation to Autonomy*, Los Angeles, CA: Semiotext(e).

Berger, P.L., 1967. *The Sacred Canopy; Elements of a Sociological Theory of Religion*, Garden City, NY: Doubleday.

Berger, P.L., Berger, B., and Kellner, H., 1973. *The Homeless Mind; Modernization and Consciousness*, New York: Random House.

Berger, P.L., Davie, G., and Fokas, E., 2008. *Religious America, Secular Europe? A Theme and Variation*, Aldershot and Burlington, VT: Ashgate Publishing, Ltd.

116   References

Berman, M., 1981. *The Reenchantment of the World*, Ithaca, NY: Cornell University Press.

Berman, M., 1988. *All That Is Solid Melts into Air: The Experience of Modernity*, New York: Penguin.

Blackmore, B., n.d. 'Church Production Magazine – About Us.' *Church Production Magazine.* Available at: www.churchproduction.com/go.php/about_us [Accessed May 7, 2010].

Bloch, E., 1972. *Atheism in Christianity: The Religion of the Exodus and the Kingdom*, New York: Herder and Herder.

Böhme, G., 1993. 'Atmosphere as the Fundamental Concept of a New Aesthetics.' *Thesis Eleven*, 36(1): 113–126.

Boltanski, L. and Chiapello, E., 2005. 'The New Spirit of Capitalism.' *International Journal of Politics, Culture, and Society*, 18(3–4): 161–188.

Borgmann, A., 2003. *Power Failure: Christianity in the Culture of Technology*, Grand Rapids, MI: Brazos Press.

Borland, J. and Kanellos, M., 2004. 'South Korea leads the way – CNET News.' *CNET News.* Available at: http://news.cnet.com/South-Korea-leads-the-way/2009-1034_3-5261393.html [Accessed August 29, 2010].

Bottici, C., 2009. 'The Politics of Imagination and the Public Role of Religion.' *Philosophy & Social Criticism*, 35(8): 985–1005.

Bottomore, S., 2002. 'Projecting for the Lord: The Work of Wilson Carlile.' *Film History*, 14(2): 195–209.

Bourdieu, P., 1984. *Distinction*, Cambridge, MA: Harvard University Press.

Boy, J., 2011. 'What We Talk about When We Talk about the Postsecular.' *The Immanent Frame: Secularism, Religion and the Public Sphere.* Available at: http://blogs.ssrc.org/tif/2011/03/15/what-we-talk-about-when-we-talk-about-the-postsecular [Accessed June 2, 2015].

Brague, R., 2004. *The Wisdom of the World: The Human Experience of the Universe in Western Thought*, Chicago, IL: University Of Chicago Press.

Brey, P., 2004. "Theorizing Modernity and Technology." In T. J. Misa, P. Brey, and A. Feenberg, eds, *Modernity and Technology*, Cambridge, MA: MIT Press: 33–71.

Bright Church, n.d., 'Facebook | Bright Church Wall.' *Facebook.* Available online.

Bright Church, 2007. 'Bright Church – About Us.' Available online.

Bright Church, 2008. 'General FAQs.' *Bright Church website.* Available online.

Bright Church, 2010. 'All Through Out the Bible God Has been for Our Neighbors. How Can you Show the Love of God to the People who Live on Your Street this Weekend?' Available online.

Brooks, D., 2010. 'The God That Fails.' *The New York Times.* Available at: www.nytimes.com/2010/01/01/opinion/01brooks.html?_r=2&hp [Accessed January 11, 2011].

Bruno, G., 2014. *Surface: Matters of Aesthetics, Materiality, and Media*, Chicago, IL: University of Chicago Press.

Buckner, B., 2010. 'Redeeming the Internet.' *Collide Magazine.* Available at: www.collidemagazine.com/article/302/redeeming-the-internet [Accessed July 7, 2010].

Bultmann, R., 1961. *Kerygma and Myth: A Theological Debate*, New York: Harper.

Bultmann, R., 1976. *History of the Synoptic Tradition*, New York: Harper.

Bultmann, R., 1980. *Jesus and the Word*, new edn, New York: Scribner.

Bunt, G.R., 2003. *Islam in the Digital Age: e-jihad, Online Fatwas and Cyber Islamic Environments*, London and Sterling, VA: Pluto Press.

References 117

Byers, D., 2010a. 'Communion: Let's Remember Together.' Available online.

Byers, D., 2010b. 'Let's Talk It Over.' Available online.

Calhoun, C., 1998. 'Community without Propinquity Revisited: Communications Technology and the Transformation of the Urban Public Sphere.' *Sociological Inquiry*, 68(3): 373–397.

Calhoun, C., 2003. "Information Technology and the International Public Sphere." In D. Schuler and P. Day, eds, *Shaping the Network Society: The New Role of Civil Society in Cyberspace*. Cambridge, MA: MIT Press: 229–251.

Calhoun, C., 2012. "Time, World and Secularism." In P. Gorskiet *et al.*, eds, *The Post-Secular in Question: Religion in Contemporary Society*. New York: NYU Press, pp. 335–364.

Campbell, H., 2004. 'Challenges Created by Online Religious Networks.' *Journal of Media and Religion*, 3(2): 81.

Campbell, H., 2005. *Exploring Religious Community Online: We Are One In The Network*, New York: Peter Lang.

Campbell, H., 2010. *When Religion Meets New Media*, London and New York: Routledge.

Campbell, H.A. ed., 2012. *Digital Religion: Understanding Religious Practice in New Media Worlds*, first edn, Abingdon and New York: Routledge.

Campbell, H.A., 2013. 'Religion and the Internet: A Microcosm for Studying Internet Trends and Implications.' *New Media & Society*, 15(5): 680–694.

Capps, M., 2008. 'Collide Magazine | Theosthetics.' *Collide Magazine.* Available at: www.collidemagazine.com/article/109/theosthetics [Accessed August 8, 2010].

Caputo, J., 1997. *The Prayers and Tears of Jacques Derrida: Religion without Religion*, Bloomington, IN: Indiana University Press.

Caputo, J., 2001. *On Religion*, Abingdon and New York: Routledge.

Caputo, J., 2007. 'Bodies Still Unrisen, Events Still Unsaid.' *Angelaki: Journal of Theoretical Humanities*, 12(1): 73.

Caputo, J.D. ed., 2001. *The Religious*, Malden, MA: Wiley-Blackwell.

Caputo, J.D. and Alcoff, L.M., 2009. *St. Paul among the Philosophers*, Bloomington, IN: Indiana University Press.

Caputo, J.D. and McLaren, B., 2007. *What Would Jesus Deconstruct? The Good News of Postmodernism for the Church*, Grand Rapids, MI: Baker Academic.

Caputo, J.D. and Scanlon, M.J. eds, 1999. *God, the Gift, and Postmodernism*, new edn, Bloomington, IN: Indiana University Press.

Carrette, J. and King, R., 2012. "Spirituality and the Re-branding of Religion." In G. Lynch, J. Mitchell, and A. Strahan, eds, *Religion, Media and Culture: A Reader.* Abingdon and New York: Routledge: 59–70.

Casanova, J., 2001. 'Religion, the New Millennium, and Globalization.' *Sociology of Religion*, 62(4): 415–441.

Casanova, J., 2008. "Public Religions Revisited." In H. De Vries, ed. *Religion Beyond a Concept.* New York: Fordham University Press: 101–119.

Casanova, J., 2012. "Trajectories of Post-secular Complexity: An Introduction." In P. Nynas, M. Lassander, and T. Utriainen, eds, *Post-Secular Society*, New Brunswick, NJ: Transaction Publishers: 27–46.

Castells, M., 1997. 'An Introduction to the Information Age.' *City*, 2(7): 6–16.

Castells, M., 2008. 'The New Public Sphere: Global Civil Society, Communication Networks, and Global Governance.' *The ANNALS of the American Academy of Political and Social Science*, 616(1): 78–93.

118   References

Chidester, D., 2003. *Salvation and Suicide: Jim Jones, the People's Temple, and Jonestown*, Bloomington, IN: Indiana University Press.

Clarke, A.C., 2000. *Profiles of the Future: An Inquiry into the Limits of the Possible*, London: Phoenix (an Imprint of The Orion Publishing Group Ltd).

Cohn, N., 2015. 'Big Drop in Share of Americans Calling Themselves Christian.' *The New York Times*. Available at: www.nytimes.com/2015/05/12/upshot/big-drop-in-share-of-americans-calling-themselves-christian.html [Accessed May 29, 2015].

Connolly, W.E., 2005. 'The Evangelical-Capitalist Resonance Machine.' *Political Theory*, 33(6): 869–886.

Couldry, N., 2004. 'Liveness, "Reality," and the Mediated Habitus from Television to the Mobile Phone.' *The Communication Review*, 7(4): 353–361.

Cox, H.G., 1965. *The Secular City: Secularization and Urbanization in Theological Perspective*, New York: Macmillan.

Cusset, F., 2008. *French Theory: How Foucault, Derrida, Deleuze, & Co. Transformed the Intellectual Life of the United States*, Minneapolis, MN: University of Minnesota Press.

David, A., 2010. 'Pope to Priests: Go Forth and Blog.' *Yahoo! News*. Available at: http://news.yahoo.com/s/ap/20100123/ap_on_re_eu/eu_pope_cyberpriests [Accessed February 5, 2010].

Davie, G., 1994. *Religion in Britain since 1945: Believing without Belonging*, Malden, MA: Wiley-Blackwell.

Davie, G., 2004. 'New Approaches in the Sociology of Religion: A Western Perspective.' *Social Compass*, 51(1): 73–84.

Dawson, L.L. and Cowan, D.E., 2004a. "Introduction." In *Religion Online: Finding Faith on the Internet*, Abingdon and New York: Routledge, pp. 1–16.

Dawson, L.L. and Cowan, D.E., 2004b. *Religion Online: Finding Faith on the Internet*, Abingdon and New York: Routledge.

Deleuze, G., 1997. 'Immanence: A Life …' *Theory Culture & society*, 14(2): 3.

Deleuze, G., 1988. *Foucault*, first edition, Minneapolis: University of Minnesota Press.

Derrida, J., 1978. "Structure, Sign and Play in the Discourse of the Human Sciences." In P. Kamuf, ed., *A Derrida Reader: Between the Blinds*. Chicago, IL: Chicago University Press: 351–350.

Derrida, J., 2002. *Acts of Religion*, London: Routledge.

Douglas, M., 1988. 'The Effects of Modernization on Religious Change.' *Daedalus*, 117(3): 457–484.

Drinnon, D., 'List of Online Churches and Internet Campuses.' *Equip Them*. Available at: www.equipthem.info/directory-of-online-churches-and-internet-campuses [Accessed July 9, 2010].

Durkheim, E., 2001. *The Elementary Forms of Religious Life*, Oxford: Oxford University Press.

Durkheim, E. and Mauss, M., 1963. *Primitive Classification*, London: Cohen & West.

Eagleton, T., 2014. *Culture and the Death of God*, New Haven, CT: Yale University Press.

Eliade, M., 1954. *The Myth of the Eternal Return*, New York: Pantheon Books.

Eliade, M., 1959. *The Sacred and the Profane: The Nature of Religion*, New York: Harcourt, Brace.

Eliade, M., 1968. *Myth and Reality Trade*, third edn, New York: HarperCollins.

Ellingson, S., 2007. *The Megachurch and the Mainline: Remaking Religious Tradition in the Twenty-first Century*, Chicago, IL: University of Chicago Press.

References 119

Ellul, J., 1964. *The Technological Society*, New York: Knopf.

Erlanger, S., 2010. 'Parliament Moves France Closer to a Ban on Facial Veils.' *The New York Times*. Available at: www.nytimes.com/2010/07/14/world/europe/14burqa. html?scp=1&sq=veil%20france&st=cse [Accessed August 4, 2010].

Evans, J.H. and Evans, M.S., 2008. 'Religion and Science: Beyond the Epistemological Conflict Narrative.' *Annual Review of Sociology*, 34(1): 87–105.

Farman, J., 2010. 'Mapping the Digital Empire: Google Earth and the Process of Postmodern Cartography.' *New Media & Society*, 12(6): 869.

Faust, B. and Faust, J., 2008. 'Jesus is Coming! (Are You Ready?).' *Living Sounds Digital Ministries*. Available at: http://livingsounds.org/newsletter/06-29-2008 [Accessed August 19, 2010].

Featherstone, M., 2014. 'Einstein's Nightmare: On Bernard Stiegler's Techno-Dystopia.' *CTheory*. Available at: www.citeulike.org/group/17991/article/13197811 [Accessed June 2, 2015].

Feenberg, A., 1991. *Critical Theory of Technology*, Oxford: Oxford University Press.

Feenberg, A., 2002. *Transforming Technology*, Oxford: Oxford University Press.

Feenberg, A., 2010. *Between Reason and Experience: Essays in Technology and Modernity*, Cambridge, MA: MIT Press.

Finke, R. and Stark, R., 2005. *The Churching of America, 1776–2005: Winners and Losers in our Religious Economy*, New Brunswick, NJ: Rutgers University Press.

Flood, G.D., 1999. *Beyond Phenomenology: Rethinking the Study of Religion*, New York: Continuum.

Foster, H., 1997. 'Prosthetic Gods.' *Modernism Modernity*, 4(2): 5–38.

Foucault, M., 1970. *The Order of Things: An Archaeology of the Human Sciences*, New York: Vintage Books.

Foucault, M., 1971. 'Orders of Discourse.' *Social Science Information*, 10(2): 7.

Friedman, T.L., 2000. *The Lexus and the Olive Tree*, New York: Macmillan.

Funkenstein, A., 1989. *Theology and the Scientific Imagination from the Middle Ages to the Seventeenth Century*, Princeton, NJ: Princeton University Press.

Gadamer, H.-G., 1977. *Philosophical Hermeneutics*, Berkeley, CA: University of California Press.

Gauchet, M., 1999. *The Disenchantment of the World*, Princeton, NJ: Princeton University Press.

Gay, D. and Rienstra, R., 2008. 'Veering Off the Via Media: Emerging Church, Alternative Worship, and New Media Technologies in the United States and United Kingdom.' *Liturgy*, 23(3): 39–47.

Geertz, C., 2004. "Religion as Cultural System." In M. Banton, ed. *Anthropological Approaches to the Study of Religion*. London: Routledge: 1–46.

Germain, G., 1993. *A Discourse on Disenchantment: Reflections on Politics and Technology*, Albany, NY: State University of New York Press.

Geroulanos, S., 2006. "Theoscopy: Transparency, Omnipotence, and Modernity." In H. de Vries and L. E. Sullivan, eds, *Political Theologies: Public Religions in a Post-secular World*. New York: Fordham University Press: 633–651.

Giddens, A., 1993. *New Rules of Sociological Method: A Positive Critique of Interpretative Sociologies*, Palo Alto, CA: Stanford University Press.

Gillespie, M.A., 2008. *The Theological Origins of Modernity*, Chicago, IL: University of Chicago Press.

Girard, R., 1977. *Violence and the Sacred*, Baltimore, MD: The Johns Hopkins University Press.

120   References

Gitelman, L., 2000. *Scripts, Grooves, and Writing Machines: Representing Technology in the Edison Era*, Stanford, CA: Stanford University Press.

Goh, R.B.H., 2008. 'Hillsong and "Megachurch" Practice: Semiotics, Spatial Logic and the Embodiment of Contemporary Evangelical Protestantism.' *Material Religion: The Journal of Objects, Art and Belief*, 4(3): 284–304.

Google maps, 'About Google Maps – Maps Help.' *Google maps*. Available at: http://maps.google.com/support/bin/answer.py?answer=7060&topic=10778 [Accessed October 19, 2010].

Gorski, P., 2008. *From the Square: Exploring the Post-Secular*. New York: NYU press.

Gorski, P., Kim, D.K., Torpey, J., and VanAntwerpen, J., 2012a. "The Post-secular in Question." In *The Post-Secular in Question: Religion in Contemporary Society*. New York: NYU Press: 1–22.

Gorski, P., Kim, D.K., Torpey, J., and VanAntwerpen, J., eds, 2012b. *The Post-Secular in Question: Religion in Contemporary Society*, New York: NYU Press.

Gravois, J., 2010. 'The Agnostic Cartographer.' *Washington Monthly*. Available at: www.washingtonmonthly.com/features/2010/1007.gravois.html [Accessed October 18, 2010].

Great Commission Research Network, 'About GCRN.' *The Great Commission Research Network*. Available at: www.ascg.org/about [Accessed August 8, 2010].

Grossman, C.L., 2009. 'Multisite Churches Mean Pastors Reach Thousands.' *USA Today*. Available at: www.usatoday.com/news/religion/2009-12-17-1Amultichurches17_CV_N.htm [Accessed July 7, 2010].

Habermas, J., 1983. "Modernity: An Incomplete Project." In H. Foster, ed., *The Anti-aesthetic: Essays on Postmodern Culture*. New York: New Press, pp. 3–15.

Habermas, J., 1985. *The Theory of Communicative Action: Lifeworld and System: A Critique of Functionalist Reason*, Boston, MA: Beacon Press.

Habermas, J., 2008. 'Notes on Post-Secular Society.' *New Perspectives Quarterly*, 25(4): 17–29.

Hall, C., 2010. 'Church … Virtually.' *Leadership Journal*. Available at: www.christianitytoday.com/le/communitylife/evangelism/churchvirtually.html?start=1 [Accessed July 9, 2010].

Han, S., 2011. *Web 2.0*, Abingdon: Routledge.

Hansen, M., 2011. 'Pope Urges Christians to Connect Online, But Not Live There.' *PCMag.com*. Available at: www.pcmag.com/article2/0,2817,2376170,00.asp [Accessed January 27, 2011].

Hansen, M.B.N., 2006. *Bodies in Code: Interfaces with Digital Media,* first edition, New York and London: Routledge.

Haraway, D., 2002. "The Persistence of Vision." In N. Mirzoeff, ed., *The Visual Culture Reader*. London and New York: Routledge: 677–684.

Harley, J.B., 1989. 'Deconstructing the Map.' *Cartographica: The International Journal for Geographic Information and Geovisualization*, 26(2): 1–20.

Harman, G., 2009. *Prince of Networks: Bruno Latour and Metaphysics*, Prahran, Victoria: Re-Press.

Hart, K., 2002. "The Experience of God." In J.D. Caputo, ed., *The Religious*. Malden, MA: Wiley-Blackwell: 159–174.

Hawking, S., 1998. *A Brief History of Time*, New York: Bantam.

Hayles, N.K., 2002. 'Flesh and Metal: Reconfiguring the Mindbody in Virtual Environments.' *Configurations*, 10(2): 297–320.

References   121

Heffernan, V., 2009. 'Uploading the Avant-Garde.' *The New York Times*. Available at: www.nytimes.com/2009/09/06/magazine/06FOB-medium-t.html?_r=1&hpw [Accessed February 3, 2010].

Heidegger, M., 1977. "The Age of the World Picture." In *The Question Concerning Technology, and Other Essays*. New York: Garland Publishing, p. xxxix.

Heidegger, M., 2001. "The Onto-theo-logical Constitution of Metaphysics." In J.D. Caputo, ed., *The Religious*. Malden, MA: Blackwell: 67–75.

Heidegger, M., 2008. *Being and Time*, New York: HarperPerennial/Modern Thought.

Helland, C., 2000. 'Online-religion/Religion-online and Virtual Communitas.' *Religion and the Social Order*, 8: 205–224.

Helland, C., 2004. "Popular Religion and the World Wide Web: A Match Made in (Cyber) Heaven." In Dawson, L.L. and Cowan, D.E., 2004b. *Religion Online: Finding Faith on the Internet*, Abingdon and New York: Routledge: 23–36.

Hendershot, H., 2004. *Shaking the World for Jesus: Media and Conservative Evangelical Culture*, Chicago, IL: University of Chicago Press.

Hendricks, K., 2008. 'The 21st-Century Potluck: Web 2.0 & the Church.' *Collide Magazine*. Available at: www.collidemagazine.com/article/40/the-21st-century-potluck-web-20-the-church [Accessed July 13, 2010].

Herberg, W., 1983. *Protestant, Catholic, Jew*, Chicago, IL: University of Chicago Press.

Hervieu-Léger, D., 2002. 'Space and Religion: New Approaches to Religious Spatiality in Modernity.' *International Journal of Urban and Regional Research*, 26(1): 99–105.

Hill, J., 2011. 'Michael Jordan, Nike, Could Do More to Stem Violence.' *ESPN.com*. Available at: http://espn.go.com/espn/commentary/story/_/id/7393317 [Accessed May 20, 2015].

Hine, C., 2007. 'Multisited Ethnography as a Middle Range Methodology for Contemporary STS.' *Science, Technology & Human Values*, 32(6): 652–671.

Hipps, S., 2006. *The Hidden Power of Electronic Culture: How Media Shapes Faith, the Gospel, and Church*, El Cajon, CA: Youth Specialties.

Hirschkind, C., 2001. 'The Ethics of Listening: Cassette-Sermon Audition in Contemporary Egypt.' *American Ethnologist*, 28(3): 623–649.

Hjarvard, S., 2008. 'The Mediatization of Religion: A Theory of the Media as Agents of Religious Change.' *Northern Lights: Film and Media Studies Yearbook*, 6(1): 9–26.

Hoover, S., 2006. *Religion in the Media Age*, London: Routledge.

Hoover, S., Clark, L.S. and Rainie, L., 2004. *Faith Online: 64% of Wired Americans Have Used the Internet for Spiritual or Religious Purposes*, Washington, DC: Pew Research Center. Available at: www.pewinternet.org/Reports/2004/Faith-Online.aspx [Accessed August 13, 2010].

Howard, R., 2006. *The Da Vinci Code*, Sony Pictures.

Howard, R.G., 2011. *Digital Jesus: The Making of a New Christian Fundamentalist Community on the Internet*, New York: NYU Press.

Husserl, E., 1970. *Crisis of European Sciences and Transcendental Phenomenology*, first edn, Evanstown, IL: Northwestern University Press.

Hutchings, T., 2012. "Creating Church Online: Networks and Collectives in Contemporary Christianity." In Gelfgren, S. *et al.*, eds, *Digital Religion, Social Media and Culture*. New York: Peter Lang Publishing, pp. 207–223.

Ihde, D., 1983. *Existential Technics*, Albany, NY: SUNY Press.

Ihde, D., 1990. *Technology and the Lifeworld: From Garden to Earth*, Bloomington, IN: Indiana University Press.

122   References

Ihde, D., 2004. "A Phenomenology of Technics." In D.M. Kaplan, ed., *Readings in the Philosophy of Technology*. New York: Rowman & Littlefield, pp. 76–97.

Ingold, T., 2000. *The Perception of the Environment: Essays on Livelihood, Dwelling and Skill*, first edn, London: Routledge.

Jacoby, S., 2010. 'Unreason in Charge in the Oil Spill Crisis.' *On Faith*. Available at: http://newsweek.washingtonpost.com/onfaith/spirited_atheist/2010/06/unreason_in_charge_in_the_oil_spill_crisis.html [Accessed January 11, 2011].

James, G.A., 1985. 'Phenomenology and the Study of Religion: The Archaeology of an Approach.' *The Journal of Religion*, 65(3): 311–335.

Jameson, F., 1988. *The Ideologies of Theory: The Syntax of History*, Minneapolis: University of Minnesota Press.

Jaspers, K., 1957. *Man in the Modern Age*, New York: Doubleday Anchor.

Jenkins, S., 2008. 'Rituals and Pixels.' *Experiments in Online Church*, 03(1). Available at: http://archiv.ub.uni-heidelberg.de/ojs/index.php/religions/article/view/390/0 [Accessed April 1, 2010].

Johnson, M., 2010. 'Worship Facilities Magazine Editorial.' *Worship Facilities Magazine*. Available at: www.worshipfacilities.com/go.php/editorial/10986 [Accessed May 10, 2010].

Kamen, A., 2008. 'One More Question ...' *Politics and Policy in Obama's Washington*. Available at: http://voices.washingtonpost.com/44/2008/12/one-more-question.html [Accessed June 24, 2010].

Kant, I., 1999. *Critique of Pure Reason*, Cambridge: Cambridge University Press.

Kavanaugh, A.L., Reese, D.D., Carroll, J.M., and Rosson, M.B., 2005. 'Weak Ties in Networked Communities.' *The Information Society*, 21(2): 119–131.

Kieckhefer, R., 1978. 'Meister Eckhart's Conception of Union with God.' *The Harvard Theological Review*, 71(3/4): 203–225.

Kittler, F.A., 1999. *Gramophone, Film, Typewriter*, Palo Alto, CA: Stanford University Press.

Kumarasamy, J., Devi Apayee, P. and Subramaniam, M., 2014. 'Emotion and Expression Responses Through Colour: A Literature Review.' Available at: http://papers.ssrn.com/sol3/papers.cfm?abstract_id=2435741 [Accessed June 2, 2015].

Kutchma, T.M., 2014. 'The Effects of Room Color on Stress Perception: Red versus Green Environments.' *Journal of Undergraduate Research at Minnesota State University, Mankato*, 3(1): 3.

Kwon, H.-Y., Kim, K.C., and Warner, R.S., eds, 2001. *Korean Americans and Their Religions: Pilgrims and Missionaries from a Different Shore*, University Park, PA: Pennsylvania State University Press.

Lash, S., 2007. 'Capitalism and Metaphysics.' *Theory, Culture & Society*, 24(5): 1–26.

Latour, B., 1993. *We Have Never been Modern*, Cambridge, MA: Harvard University Press.

Latour, B., 1999. *Pandora's Hope: Essays on the Reality of Science Studies*, first edn, Cambridge, MA: Harvard University Press.

Latour, B., 2004. 'Whose Cosmos, which Cosmopolitics?: Comments on the Peace Terms of Ulrich Beck.' *Common Knowledge*, 10(3): 450.

Latour, B., 2007. 'Can We Get Our Materialism Back, Please?' *Isis*, 98(1): 138–142.

Latour, B., 2008. "A Cautious Prometheus? A Few Steps Toward a Philosophy of Design (with Special Attention to Peter Sloterdijk)." In *Proceedings of the 2008 Annual International Conference of the Design History Society*, Boca Raton, CA: Universal Publishers, pp. 2–10.

References 123

Latour, B., 2011. 'Networks, Societies, Spheres: Reflections of an Actor-network Theorist.' *International Journal of Communication*, 5: 796–810.

Lauretis, T.D., 1984. *Alice Doesn't: Feminism, Semiotics, Cinema*, Bloomington, IN: Indiana University Press.

Law, J., 2004. *After Method: Mess in Social Science Research*, London and New York: Routledge.

Lemert, C., 1975. 'Social Structure and the Absent Center: An Alternative to the New Sociologies of Religion.' *Sociological Analysis*, 36(2): 95–107.

Lemert, C., 1979. 'Science, Religion and Secularization.' *Sociological Quarterly*, 20(4): 445–461.

Lemert, C., 1980. *Sociology and the Twilight of Man: Homocentrism and Discourse in Sociological Theory*, Carbondale, IL: Southern Illinois University Press.

Lemert, C.C., 2006. *Durkheim's Ghosts*, Cambridge: Cambridge University Press.

Lessig, L., 2008. *Remix*, New York: Penguin.

Lévi-Strauss, C., 1983. *Structural Anthropology*, Chicago, IL: University of Chicago Press.

Lévinas, E., 1996. "Is Ontology Fundamental?" In A. T. Peperzak, S. Critchley, and R. Bernasconi, eds, *Emmanuel Lévinas: Basic Philosophical Writings*. Bloomington, IN: Indiana University Press, pp. 1–10.

Levinson, P., 1999. *Digital McLuhan: A Guide to the Information Millennium*, London and New York: Routledge.

Lévy, P., 2001. *Cyberculture*, Minneapolis, MA: University of Minnesota Press.

Lévy-Bruhl, L., authorized translation by L.A.C., 1966. *Primitive Mentality*, Boston, MA: Beacon Press.

Lowith, K., 1957. *Meaning in History: The Theological Implications of the Philosophy of History*, Chicago, IL: University of Chicago Press.

Luckmann, T., 1990. 'Shrinking Transcendence, Expanding Religion?' *Sociological Analysis*, 51(2): 127–138.

Ludden, J., 2005. 'Big Churches Use Technology to Branch Out: NPR.' *NPR*. Available at: www.npr.org/templates/story/story.php?storyId=4788676 [Accessed May 5, 2010].

Lukács, G., 1972. *History and Class Consciousness: Studies in Marxist Dialectics*, Cambridge, MA: MIT Press.

Lurie, A., 2003. 'God's Houses Part II.' *The New York Review of Books*. Available at: www.nybooks.com/articles/archives/2003/jul/17/gods-houses-part-ii [Accessed May 10, 2010].

Luther, M., 1958. *Martin Luther: Selections from His Writings*, New York: Anchor.

Lynch, G., 2007. *Between Sacred and Profane: Researching Religion and Popular Culture*, London and New York: I.B. Tauris.

Lynch, G. and Mitchell, J.P., 2012. *Religion, Media and Culture: A Reader*, London and New York: Routledge.

MacAngus, D., 2010. 'Interview with author.'

Maffesoli, M., 1996a. *Ordinary Knowledge: An Introduction to Interpretative Sociology*, Cambridge: Polity Press.

Maffesoli, M., 1996b. *The Contemplation of the World*, Minneapolis, MN: University of Minnesota Press.

Maffesoli, M., 1996c. *The Time of the Tribes,* first edn, London and Thousand Oaks, CA: Sage.

Mahan, J.H., 2014. *Media, Religion and Culture: An Introduction*, first edn, London and New York: Routledge.

124 References

Malinowski, B., 1954. *Magic, Science and Religion: And Other Essays*, Garden City, NY: Doubleday.

Marcel, G., 1962. *Man Against Mass Society*, Chicago, IL: H. Regnery.

Marcus, G.E. and Fischer, M.M.J., 1999. "A Crisis of Representation in the Human Sciences." In *Anthropology as Cultural Critique: An Experimental Moment in the Human Sciences*. Chicago, IL: University of Chicago Press, pp. 7–16.

Marcuse, H., 2002. *One-dimensional Man: Studies in the Ideology of Advanced Industrial Society*, London: Routledge.

Marion, J.-L., 1995. *God without Being: Hors-texte*, Chicago, IL: University of Chicago Press.

Maritain, J., 2006. *Introduction to Philosophy*, Lanham, MD: Rowman & Littlefield.

Martin, D., 1993. *Tongues of Fire: The Explosion of Protestantism in Latin America*, Malden, MA: Blackwell.

Martin, D., 2005. *On Secularization: Towards A Revised General Theory*, London: Ashgate Publishing.

Marx, L., 1964. *The Machine in the Garden: Technology and the Pastoral Ideal in America. Leo Marx*, New York: Oxford University Press.

Marx, K. and Engels, F., 1936. *Capital: A Critique of Political Economy*, New York: Modern Library.

Mauss, M., 1992. "Techniques of the Body." In J. Crary and S. Kwinter, eds, *Incorporations*. New York: Zone Books, pp. 455–477.

McClellan, S., 2009. 'Collide Magazine | Online Community At LifeChurch.tv.' *Collide Magazine*. Available at: www.collidemagazine.com/article/174/online-comm unity-at-lifechurchtv [Accessed July 12, 2010].

McLuhan, M., 1969. *The Gutenberg Galaxy*, New York: Signet.

Merton, R.K., 1938. 'Social Structure and Anomie.' *American Sociological Review*, 3(5): 672–682.

Metzger, P., 2009. 'Walls do Talk.' *Leadership Journal*. Available at: www.christianity today.com/le/buildingleaders/equipping/wallsdotalk.html [Accessed August 8, 2010].

Meyer, B., 2006. 'Religious Revelation, Secrecy and the Limits of Visual Representation.' *Anthropological Theory*, 6(4): 431–453.

Meyer, B., 2010. 'Aesthetics of Persuasion: Global Christianity and Pentecostalism's Sensational Forms.' *South Atlantic Quarterly*, 109(4): 741–763.

Miczek, N., 2008. 'Online Rituals in Virtual Worlds. Christian Online Service between Dynamics and Stability.' *Online – Heidelberg Journal of Religions on the Internet*, 3(1).

Milbank, J., 1990. *Theology and Social Theory: Beyond Secular Reason*, Oxford: Blackwell.

Milbank, J., 2003. *Being Reconciled: Ontology and Pardon*, London: Routledge.

Mills, C.W., 1953. *White Collar: The American Middle Classes*, Oxford: Oxford University Press.

Min, P.G. and Kim, J.H., 2002. *Religions in Asian America: Building Faith Communities*, Walnut Creek, CA: AltaMira Press.

Moberg, M. and Granholm, K., 2012. "The Concept of the Post-secular and the Contemporary Nexus of Religion, Media, Popular Culture and Consumer Culture." In P. Nynas, M. Lassander, and T. Utriainen, eds, *Post-Secular Society*. New Brunswick, NJ: Transaction Publishers, pp. 95–128.

Moberg, M., Granholm, K. and Nynas, P., 2012. "Trajectories of Post-secular Complexity: An Introduction." In P. Nynas, M. Lassander, and T. Utriainen, eds, *Post-Secular Society*. New Brunswick, NJ: Transaction Publishers, pp. 1–26.

References 125

Morgan, D., 2007. *The Lure of Images*, London and New York: Routledge.

Mumford, L., 1967. *The Myth of the Machine*, New York: Harcourt.

Mydans, S., 2010. 'Churches Attacked in Malaysian "Allah" Dispute.' *The New York Times*. Available at: www.nytimes.com/2010/01/09/world/asia/09malaysia.html?_r=1&scp=1&sq=malaysia%20allah&st=cse [Accessed August 4, 2010].

Nancy, J.-L., 1991. *Inoperative Community*, Minneapolis, MN: University of Minnesota Press.

Nancy, J.-L., 2007. *The Creation of the World, or, Globalization*, Albany, NY: State University of New York Press.

Nancy, J.-L., 2008a. *Dis-Enclosure: The Deconstruction of Christianity*, New York: Fordham University Press.

Nancy, J.-L., 2008b. *Noli me tangere: On the Raising of the Body*, New York: Fordham University Press.

Neil, A., 2010. 'Interview with author.'

Neumann, B. and Zierold, M., 2010. "Media as Ways of Worldmaking: Media-specific Structures and Intermedial Dynamics." In V. Nünning, V. Nunning, and A. Nunning, eds, *Cultural Ways of Worldmaking: Media and Narratives*. New York: De Gruyter, pp. 103–118.

New York Times, 1923. 'Churches to Use Radio to Reach Millions.' *New York Times*, p. 5.

Newell, G., 2011. 'Positioning a Brand: How Nike Built a Brand with Universal Appeal.' *602 Communications*. Available at: http://602communications.com/2011/11/positioning-a-brand-how-nike-built-a-brand-with-universal-appeal [Accessed May 20, 2015].

Neyrat, F. and Stiegler, B., 2012. 'Interview: From Libidinal Economy to the Ecology of the Spirit.' *Parrhesia*, 14: 9–15.

Nielsen, D.A., 1992. 'Review: Theology and Social Theory: Beyond Secular Reason by John Milbank.' *Sociological Analysis*, 53(4): 468–470.

Nietzsche, F.W., 2010. *On the Genealogy of Morals and Ecce Homo*, New York: Random House.

Noble, D.F., 1999. *The Religion of Technology: The Divinity of Man and the Spirit of Invention*, New York: Penguin Books.

Nynas, P., Lassander, M. and Utriainen, T. eds, 2012. *Post-Secular Society*, New Brunswick, NJ: Transaction Publishers.

O'Brien, C., 2013. 'How Steve Jobs and Apple Turned Technology into a Religion.' *Los Angeles Times*. Available at: http://articles.latimes.com/2013/sep/01/business/la-fi-tn-how-steve-jobs-and-apple-turned-technology-into-our-religion-20130829 [Accessed May 19, 2015].

O'Leary, S.D., 1996. 'Cyberspace as Sacred Space: Communicating Religion on Computer Networks.' *Journal of the American Academy of Religion*, 64(4): 781–808.

O'Leary, S.D., 2004. "Cyberspace as Sacred Space: Communicating Religion on Computer Networks." In *Religion Online: Finding Faith on the Internet*. London: Routledge, pp. 37–58.

O'Neill, J., 1988. 'Religion and Postmodernism: The Durkheimian Bond in Bell and Jameson.' *Theory, Culture & Society*, 5(2/3): 493–508.

Oh, M., 2005. *Bling Bling: Hip Hop's Crown Jewels*, New York: Wenner Books.

Orsi, R.A., 2002. *The Madonna of 115th Street: Faith and Community in Italian Harlem, Second Edition*, New Haven, CT: Yale University Press.

Out of Ur, 2009. 'Internet Campuses: A Blessing or Bogus?' *Out of Ur*. Available at: www.outofur.com/archives/2009/08/internet_campus.html [Accessed July 9, 2010].

126   *References*

Paley, W., 1963. *Natural Theology; Selections*, Indianapolis, IN: Bobbs-Merrill.

Parikka, J., 2012. *What is Media Archaeology*, Cambridge and Malden, MA: Polity.

Parr, B., 2010. 'Pope's Message to Priests: We Must Blog.' *Mashable*. Available at: http://mashable.com/2010/01/24/pope-priests-blog [Accessed January 27, 2011].

Pickstock, C.J.C., 2010. 'Liturgy and the Senses.' *South Atlantic Quarterly*, 109(4): 719–739.

Poster, M., 2001. *What's the Matter with the Internet?* Minneapolis, MN: University of Minnesota Press.

Rawls, J., 1985. 'Justice as Fairness: Political not Metaphysical.' *Philosophy and Public Affairs*, 14(3): 223–251.

Rawls, J., 1987. 'The Idea of an Overlapping Consensus.' *Oxford Journal of Legal Studies*, 7(1): 1–25.

Renewed Vision, 'Renewed Vision – ProPresenter 4 (Mac & PC / Windows).' *Renewed Vision*. Available at: www.renewedvision.com/propresenter.php [Accessed August 6, 2010].

Robinson, B.T., 2013. *Appletopia: Media Technology and the Religious Imagination of Steve Jobs*, Waco, TX: Baylor University Press.

Roof, W.C., 2001. *Spiritual Marketplace: Baby Boomers and the Remaking of American Religion*, Princeton, NJ: Princeton University Press.

Rosen-Molina, M., 2009. 'Religious Evangelists Spread Faith through Social Media.' *MediaShift*. Available at: www.pbs.org/mediashift/2009/06/religious-evangelists-spread-faith-through-social-media155.html [Accessed June 14, 2010].

Roy, R., 2002. 'Religion/Technology, Not Theology/Science, as the Defining Dichotomy.' *Zygon*, 37(3): 667–676.

Russell, B., 2010. 'What Lion Are You Chasing?' Available online.

Scheler, M., 2011. *The Nature of Sympathy*, New Brunswick, NJ and London: Transaction Publishers.

Schneider, N., 2012. 'How Occupy Wall Street got Religion.' *Waging Nonviolence*. Available at: http://wagingnonviolence.org/feature/how-occupy-wall-street-got-religion [Accessed May 28, 2015].

Scott, J., 1989. 'Prestige as the Public Discourse of Domination.' *Cultural Critique*, 12: 145–166.

Shilling, C. and Mellor, P.A., 2001. *The Sociological Ambition: Elementary Forms of Social and Moral Life*, London: Thousand Oaks, CA: SAGE.

Shirky, C., 2002. 'In-Room Chat as a Social Tool.' *O'Reilly P2P*. Available at: http://openp2p.com/lpt/a/3071 [Accessed June 15, 2010].

Simpson, B., 2009. 'Collide Magazine | Gathered, Yet Mediated.' *Collide Magazine*. Available at: www.collidemagazine.com/article/195/gathered-yet-mediated [Accessed July 12, 2010].

Simpson, B., 2010. 'The Power of Awe: The Affections and Christian Existence.' *Collide Magazine*. Available at: www.collidemagazine.com/article/309/the-power-of-awe-the-affections-and-christian-existence [Accessed August 8, 2010].

Singer, P., 2004. *One World: The Ethics of Globalization*, New Haven, CT: Yale University Press.

Sitz, J., 2010. 'Interview with author.'

Sloterdijk, P., 2004. 'Anthropo-Technology.' *New Perspectives Quarterly*, 21(4): 40–44.

Sloterdijk, P., 2005. "Foreword to the Theory of Spheres." In Ohanian, M. and Royaux, J.C. eds, *Cosmograms*, New York: Lukas and Sternberg, pp. 223–240.

References 127

Sloterdijk, P., 2009a. 'Geometry in the Colossal: The Project of Metaphysical Globalization.' *Environment and Planning D: Society and Space*, 27(1): 29–40.

Sloterdijk, P., 2009b. 'Spheres Theory: Talking to Myself About the Poetics of Space.' *Harvard Design Magazine*, Spring/Summer (30): 126–137.

Sloterdijk, P., 2011. *Bubbles: Spheres Volume I: Microspherology*, Los Angeles, CA: Semiotext(e).

Smith, C., 2003. *Moral, Believing Animals: Human Personhood and Culture*, Oxford: Oxford University Press.

Smith, C. and Emerson, M., 1998. *American Evangelicalism: Embattled and Thriving*, Chicago, IL: University of Chicago Press.

Smith, J., 2009. 'Facebook to Launch Redesigned Pages for Businesses – Tour & First Impressions.' *Inside Facebook: Tracking Facebook and the Facebook Platform for Developers and Marketers.* Available at: www.insidefacebook.com/2009/02/16/facebook-to-launch-redesigned-pages-for-businesses-tour-first-impressions [Accessed June 19, 2010].

Son, W.-C., 2010. 'Overcoming the Technological Divide.' *The Global Conversation.* Available at: www.christianitytoday.com/globalconversation/june2010/response2.html [Accessed July 14, 2010].

Soukup, P.A., 1999. 'On-Line Religion: A New Context for Religious Practice.' *America* 180(6): 8–10.

Stark, R. and Finke, R., 2000. *Acts of Faith: Explaining the Human Side of Religion*, Berkeley, CA: University of California Press.

Stiegler, B., 1998. *Technics and Time*, Stanford, CA: Stanford University Press.

Stiegler, B., 2013. *Uncontrollable Societies of Disaffected Individuals: Disbelief and Discredit*, Cambridge: Polity.

Stiegler, B., 2014. *The Re-Enchantment of the World: The Value of Spirit Against Industrial Populism*, New York: Bloomsbury.

Stolow, J., 2005. 'Religion and/as Media.' *Theory, Culture & Society*, 22(4): 119–145.

Stolow, J., 2013. *Deus in Machina: Religion, Technology, and the Things in between*, New York: Fordham University Press.

Stout, D.A., 2011. *Media and Religion: Foundations of an Emerging Field*, New York: Routledge.

Surratt, G., 2009. 'An Inside Look at the Multisite Movement.' *Collide Magazine.* Available at: www.collidemagazine.com/article/287/an-inside-look-at-the-multi-site-movement [Accessed August 9, 2010].

Surratt, G., Ligon, G. and Bird, W., 2009. *A Multi-Site Church Roadtrip: Exploring the New Normal,* first edn, Grand Rapids, MI: Zondervan.

Szerszynski, B., 2005. *Nature, Technology and the Sacred*, Malden, MA: Wiley-Blackwell.

Taylor, C., 1992. *Sources of the Self: The Making of the Modern Identity*, Cambridge: Cambridge University Press.

Taylor, C., 2003. "Closed World Structures." In M.A. Wrathall, ed., *Religion After Metaphysics*. Cambridge: Cambridge University Press, pp. 47–68.

Taylor, C., 2007. *A Secular Age*, Cambridge, MA: Belknap Press of Harvard University Press.

Taylor, C., 2011. "Disenchantment–Renchantment." In G. Levine, ed., *The Joy of Secularism: 11 Essays for How We Live Now*. Princeton, NJ: Princeton University Press, pp. 57–73.

Taylor, M.C., 2007. *After God*, Chicago, IL: University of Chicago Press.

128   References

Thomas, S., 2008a. 'Pictures of the GOC 2.0.' *What's on My Mind at the Moment*. Available at: http://sunnythomas.net/2008/05/18/pictures-of-the-goc-20 [Accessed August 8, 2010].

Thomas, S., 2008b. 'What's the GOC?' *What's on My Mind at the Moment*. Available at: http://sunnythomas.net/2008/05/18/whats-the-goc [Accessed August 8, 2010].

Thompson, C., 2007. 'Clive Thompson on How Twitter Creates a Social Sixth Sense.' *Wired*, 15(07). Available at: www.wired.com/techbiz/media/magazine/15-07/st_thompson [Accessed July 13, 2010].

Thompson, J.B., 1995. *The Media and Modernity: A Social Theory of the Media*, Stanford, CA: Stanford University Press.

Thompson, P., 2009. 'Worship Facilities Magazine Editorial.' *Worship Facilities Magazine*. Available at: www.worshipfacilities.com/go.php/editorial/8744 [Accessed May 7, 2010].

Thrift, N., 2007. *Non-Representational Theory: Space, Politics, Affect*, London: Routledge.

Thumma, S. and Bird, W., 2008. *Changes in American Megachurches: Tracing Eight Years of Growth and Innovation in the Nation's Largest-Attendance Congregations*, Hartford, CT: Hartford Seminary, Hartford Institute of Religion Research.

Thumma, S., and Travis, D., 2007. *Beyond Megachurch Myths: What We Can Learn from America's Largest Churches*, San Francisco, CA: Jossey-Bass.

Tönnies, F., 2002. *Community and Society*, Mineola, NY: Dover Publications.

Toppa, S., 2015. 'These Cities Have The Worst Traffic in the World.' *Time*. Available at: http://time.com/3695068/worst-cities-traffic-jams [Accessed May 3, 2015].

Torpey, J., 2010. 'A (Post-) Secular Age? Religion and the Two Exceptionalisms.' *Social Research*, 77(1): 269–296.

Toscano, A., 2007. 'Vital Strategies: Maurizio Lazzarato and the Metaphysics of Contemporary Capitalism.' *Theory, Culture and Society*, 24(6): 71–91.

Trenholm, R., 2011. 'Apple Stimulates Brain's Religious Responses, Claims BBC.' *CNET*. Available at: www.cnet.com/uk/news/apple-stimulates-brains-religious-responses-claims-bbc [Accessed May 19, 2015].

Turner, B., 2008. 'Religious Speech: The Ineffable Nature of Religious Communication.' *Theory, Culture & Society*, 25(7–8): 219.

Turner, B., 2012. "Post-Secular Society: Consumerism and the Democratization of Religion." In P. Gorski *et al.*, eds, *The Post-Secular in Question: Religion in Contemporary Society*. New York: NYU Press, pp. 135–158.

Turner, R.H., 1956. 'Role-taking, Role Standpoint, and Reference-group Behavior.' *American Journal of Sociology*, 61(4): 316–328.

Vattimo, G., 1999. *Belief*, Palo Alto, CA: Stanford University Press.

Vattimo, G., 2002. *After Christianity*, New York: Columbia University Press.

Vattimo, G. and Caputo, J.D., 2013. *After the Death of God*, New York: Columbia University Press.

Vitello, P., 2009. 'Lead Us to Tweet, and Forgive the Trespassers.' *The New York Times*. Available at: www.nytimes.com/2009/07/05/technology/internet/05twitter.html?_r=1&hp=&pagewanted=print [Accessed June 15, 2010].

De Vries, H., 1999. *Philosophy and the Turn to Religion*, Baltimore, Md.: The Johns Hopkins University Press.

De Vries, H. and Weber, S. eds, 2002. *Religion and Media*, first edition, Palo Alto, CA: Stanford University Press.

Ward, G., 1997. *The Postmodern God: A Theological Reader*, Malden: Wiley-Blackwell.

References   129

Ward, G., 2006. 'The Future of Religion.' *Journal of the American Academy of Religion*, 74(1): 179.

Webb, B., 2009. 'Worship Facilities Magazine Editorial.' *Worship Facilities Magazine.* Available at: www.worshipfacilities.com/go.php/editorial/8932 [Accessed May 7, 2010].

Weber, M., 1958. 'Science as a Vocation.' *Daedalus*, 87(1): 111–134.

Weber, M., 1991. "Science as a Vocation." In H. Gerth and C. W. Mills, eds, *From Max Weber: Essays in Sociology.* London: Routledge.

Weber, S. and Cholodenko, A., 1996. *Mass Mediauras*, Stanford, CA: Stanford University Press.

White, L.T., 1968. *Machina ex deo: Essays in the Dynamism of Western Culture*, Cambridge, MA: MIT Press.

White, S., 1994. *Christian Worship and Technological Change*, Nashville, IN: Abingdon Press.

Wilkie, A., 2010. 'User Assemblages in Design: An Ethnographic Study.' Doctoral. London: Goldsmiths, University of London. Available at: http://research.gold.ac.uk/4710 [Accessed May 23, 2015].

Wilson, B.R., 1998. "The Secularization Thesis: Criticisms and Rebuttals." In Laermans, R., Wilson, B.R., and Billiet, J., eds, *Secularization and Social Integration: Papers in Honor of Karel Dobbelaere.* Leuven: Leuven University Press, pp. 45–66.

Wood, D., 2003. 'Albert Borgmann on Taming Technology: An Interview.' *The Christian Century*, 120(17): 22–25.

Wood, J., 2011. 'Is That All There Is?: Secularism and its Discontents.' *The New Yorker.* Available at: www.newyorker.com/arts/critics/atlarge/2011/08/15/110815crat_atlarge_wood [Accessed November 29, 2011].

Wrathall, M.A., 2003. "Introduction: Metaphysics and Onto-theology." In M.A. Wrathall, ed., *Religion After Metaphysics.* Cambridge: Cambridge University Press, pp. 1–6.

Wuthnow, R., 1993. 'Small Groups Forge New Notions of Community and the Sacred'. *The Christian Century*, 110(35): 1236–1240.

Wuthnow, R., 1998. *After Heaven: Spirituality in America Since the 1950s*, first edn, Berkeley, CA: University of California Press.

Wuthnow, R., 2003. *Creative Spirituality: The Way of the Artist*, Berkeley, CA: University of California Press.

Young, G., 2004. "Reading and Praying Online: The Continuity of Religion Online and Online Religion in Internet Christianity." In *Religion Online: Finding Faith on the Internet.* London: Routledge, pp. 93–106.

Zielinski, S., 2008. *Deep Time of the Media: Toward an Archaeology of Hearing and Seeing by Technical Means*, Cambridge, MA: MIT Press.

Index

(atmo)sphere 54, 65–7, 71–2
aesthetics 50, 57, 66–9, 71–3, 111; and liturgy 51, 58, 67, 79, 81
affect 12, 43, 48, 54–5, 57, 59, 65–70, 86–8, 100, 105–7
Apple 99, 105–7, 112
Asad, Talal 6, 18–19, 84–5, 91–2
assemblage 13, 30, 48

belief 7, 13, 24, 26, 46–8, 53, 67, 76–7, 84–5, 100–1
Bell, Daniel 109–110
Berardi, Franco "Bifo" 104–5
Berger, Peter 5, 14, 31–6, 39, 41–3
body 9–10, 40–1, 67–8, 71–2, 83–4
Bright Church 14–15, 57–63, 68–9, 72–5, 78–84, 86–8
bubbles: *see* spheres

Campbell, Heidi 7–8, 76–7, 84–5,
capitalism 47–8, 90–1, 98–105; and spirituality 102–103, 107
classical social theory 4, 76
cognitive capitalism 100, 104
community 3, 7, 9, 12, 14, 53–4, 58, 71–2, 76–8, 80–5, 87–89, 111–12
consumerism 71, 95, 101–3, 105, 107, 110–13
cosmos 25, 33–6, 42–3, 108–9

design 13, 54–7, 67–8, 70–1
disenchantment 14, 16, 18–20, 23, 25–27, 100
Divine Clockmaker 29–30, 44
Durkheim, Emile 4, 31–2, 36, 76, 85–7, 112

Eliade, Mircea 14, 31, 34–6, 41, 43
emotion 67, 69–71, 86–8, 103, 105

enchantment 101, 112
Enlightenment 3–4, 25, 85, 93, 97, 106
environment 12, 14–15, 20, 24, 26–7, 31, 37, 39, 54, 58–59, 64–7, 73, 75–7
epistemology 33, 93, 95
ethnography 12–14

Facebook 62, 75, 78, 81–4, 86–7
feeling 65–6, 70–2, 86–7, 105, 107
fellowship 25, 58, 77, 80, 83
French sociology 3–4
Freud, Sigmund 11, 45, 101, 110
Friedman, Thomas 26–8

Geertz, Clifford 5–6
German sociology 3–4
Graphic User Interface(GUI) 78

Habermas, Jurgen 10, 17, 96–7
Heidegger, Martin 3, 14, 16, 31, 37–42, 87, 93–5, 98
Hjarvard, Stieg: see mediatization
humanism 4–7, 19–23, 25–27, 29–35, 37, 39–41, 55–6, 91–2, 94

ideology 6, 34, 47, 76
IMAG 61, 65
immanence 45, 71
immaterial labor 100, 104–7,
institutional religion 9, 53, 74
Internet 1–2, 8, 10, 27, 74–78, 80, 85, 88

Lazzarato, Maurizio 104
lifestyle 99, 103, 105, 111–12
lifeworld 13–14, 39–43
lived religion 42, 77, 88, 107
liveness 78, 84
Luckmann, Thomas 104, 108–9

Index 131

Maffesoli, Michel 69–72, 86–7
magic 23–25, 27
Marx, Karl 6, 18, 76, 98–99, 104–5,
meaning 4–6, 8, 34, 43, 45–6, 77, 92, 94, 108,
110; *see also* symbols; *see also* culture
mediatization 8–10
megachurch 3, 50–2, 54, 58, 65, 103
metaphysics 4, 16, 21–2, 26, 28, 38, 44,
56, 90, 104, 107; metaphysical
capitalism 98–100, 104, 107–8
Milbank, John 4–6, 12, 36, 41
modernist settlement 25–7
morality 4, 76, 86, 95–6, 99, 110
multi-site 12–13, 52, 57
myth of modernization 17, 22, 25–6, 92, 111

network 12, 15, 30–1, 46–9, 52–7, 77–8,
82–4, 86–9
Nike 55, 99, 105, 107, 112
nomos 32, 43
nonhuman 25–6, 55

official religion: *see* lived religion
online religion (as opposed to religion
online) 8, 10
onto-cosmology 19–20, 25, 30

participation 12, 43, 68, 72, 75–8, 97–9
phenomenology 6, 41
post-modern 12, 45, 86, 91, 96, 102, 112
post-secular 2–3, 12, 15, 90–1, 93, 95–8,
102, 104, 107–8, 112
proprioception 82–4
proxemics 78, 85–9

rationalization 14, 18–27, 109–10
religious affiliation 1–2, 9, 17, 50, 102
ritual 8–10, 19, 22, 36, 71, 76, 86–7

sacrament 85–7
sacred 31, 33–6, 76, 88–9, 108–13
science 18–20, 23–5, 29–30, 32–3, 38–9,
96–8, 102, 106, 109, 112
scientific knowledge 3–4, 6, 23–4, 29–30,
37, 97
secular modernity 2–7, 10–12, 14, 16–20,
22, 25, 27, 76, 91–2, 96–9, 103
secularism 7, 10–11, 14, 90–1, 93, 97–8
secularization theory 2, 17–19, 25, 27,
85, 91, 95–8, 100, 103, 109–10
senses 41, 43, 47–8, 66–74, 87–8, 111
sermon 58, 61–2, 75, 79, 81
Sloterdijk, Peter 14, 31, 42–4, 45, 54–7
sociology of religion 3, 5–6, 13, 30–1,
36, 52, 90, 107
space 15, 34–6, 39–40, 43–4, 50, 53–8,
66–9, 72, 86
soul 4, 93–4, 96, 104, 109
spheres 12–13, 43, 57, 66–7
Stiegler, Bernard 100–1, 105

Taylor, Charles 22, 76, 91–3
technological modernity 19–22, 25, 27–8
technological rationality 19–22
technoscience 18, 25, 95–6
transcendence 4, 65, 72, 96, 98, 108–9
Twitter 3, 78–9, 81–4

Vattimo, Gianni 95–6

Weber, Max 4, 14, 18–24, 27, 76, 98–9,
109–10
world 5–7, 13–14, 29–49, 57, 83
worship space 15, 50, 53–4, 57–8, 60,
62–5, 67–8, 72–3, 78–9

eBooks
from Taylor & Francis

Helping you to choose the right eBooks for your Library

Add to your library's digital collection today with Taylor & Francis eBooks. We have over 50,000 eBooks in the Humanities, Social Sciences, Behavioural Sciences, Built Environment and Law, from leading imprints, including Routledge, Focal Press and Psychology Press.

Choose from a range of subject packages or create your own!

Benefits for you
- Free MARC records
- COUNTER-compliant usage statistics
- Flexible purchase and pricing options
- 70% approx of our eBooks are now DRM-free.

Benefits for your user
- Off-site, anytime access via Athens or referring URL
- Print or copy pages or chapters
- Full content search
- Bookmark, highlight and annotate text
- Access to thousands of pages of quality research at the click of a button.

Free Trials Available

We offer free trials to qualifying academic, corporate and government customers.

eCollections

Choose from 20 different subject eCollections, including:

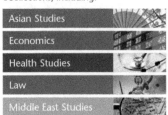

- Asian Studies
- Economics
- Health Studies
- Law
- Middle East Studies

eFocus

We have 16 cutting-edge interdisciplinary collections, including:

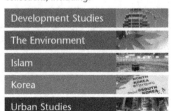

- Development Studies
- The Environment
- Islam
- Korea
- Urban Studies

For more information, pricing enquiries or to order a free trial, please contact your local sales team:

UK/Rest of World: **online.sales@tandf.co.uk**
USA/Canada/Latin America: **e-reference@taylorandfrancis.com**
East/Southeast Asia: **martin.jack@tandf.com.sg**
India: **journalsales@tandfindia.com**

www.tandfebooks.com